College and Career Readiness
MENTOR TOOLKIT

Created by Take Stock in Children

Contents

WELCOME TO THE COLLEGE AND CAREER READINESS MENTOR TOOLKIT!

AS A MENTOR, YOU HAVE CHOSEN TO MAKE A DIFFERENCE in the life of an adolescent who will benefit tremendously from one of the most precious commodities we have in the fast-moving lifestyle of today: time with a caring, supportive adult. Your direct involvement with your mentee can help shape their aspirations and realize their most deep-seeded life goals. Research has repeatedly shown the positive impact a relationship with an effective mentor can have on a student's ability to achieve, both in school and in life. The College and Career Readiness Mentor Toolkit can serve as a valuable resource towards this pursuit.

This toolkit was authored by Take Stock in Children (TSIC), a nonprofit organization that provides college and career readiness programming to over 15,000 Florida high-school and post-secondary students annually. TSIC developed this curriculum as a resource for the thousands of mentors who volunteer each year, providing them with a menu of targeted, sequenced activities they could use to engage with their mentee, build trust, and develop their mentee's awareness of the knowledge and skills necessary to achieve their college and career goals. The activities are based on the best practices and findings of interviews and focused discussions conducted with educators, university personnel, and experts in the field of mentoring and education. It is important to note that the mentee's safety and security is paramount and should always be kept at the forefront throughout the mentoring relationship. This toolkit should only be used to compliment an existing system to ensure mentee safety and security, not to supersede it.

To date, Take Stock in Children has served over 32,000 students, consistently producing remarkable results. The organization has a statewide reach that is currently unmatched by any other mentoring and college readiness organization in the United States, with affiliates serving all 67 Florida counties. The organization is also one of the nation's most well-established public-private ventures. Since 1995, Take Stock in Children has given out over $225 million in scholarships to deserving low-income students. For more on Take Stock in Children, go to www.takestockinchildren.org.

How to Use the College and Career Readiness Mentor Toolkit

The College and Career Readiness Mentor Toolkit includes activities designed to be completed within one mentoring session. Each activity provides an objective, a list of materials needed, instructions, and space for written responses. The activities are presented in a logical, sequential way; however, you may choose to select activities out of sequence, as your mentee's individual needs or interests change. Mentees will be encouraged to explore their strengths and limitations and will be guided through the full range of skills and information needed to pursue academic and career goals. You are encouraged to review each section with your mentee and decide where to start.

Your primary task as a mentor is to meet regularly with your mentee. Mentees should be encouraged, but not forced, to talk about such things as preparing for college and planning for a career. The two most important things mentors can do for their mentees are to listen to their thoughts and feelings without judgment and provide support and resources for achieving their goals, whatever they may be.

The curriculum contained in this toolkit is divided into eight sections:

1) **Personal Growth and Development** – *This section is designed to help mentors and mentees get to know each other by exploring personal interests and preferences and identifying commonalities. It also includes activities that will help mentees establish their academic and career goals, as well as focus their attention on the positive values that will help them succeed in school and in life.*

2) **Social-Emotional Learning** – *This section is designed for mentors interested in helping their mentees further develop their social-emotional skills. It includes an introduction to social-emotional learning, as well as activities designed specifically to address the 5 primary components of social-emotional learning.*

3) **Supporting Academic Success** – *This section includes activities that will help mentors model and teach their mentees the skills that will best support their academic success, such as task organization, effective note-taking, and test preparation.*

4) **College Readiness** – *The activities in this section will assist mentors with preparing their mentees for the college application process, including choosing the right school, understanding the types of degrees available, and applying for financial aid.*

5) **Career Readiness** – *Using the activities in this section, mentors will guide mentees through the process of identifying their career interests, as well as build the skills needed to successfully navigate a job search, including building a resume and interviewing with potential employers.*

6) **Road Map to College** – *This section of this toolkit includes checklists mentors can use with their mentees during middle school and then each year of high school, to ensure they are taking the actions necessary at each stage to successfully graduate high school on time and enroll in the post-secondary program of their choosing.*

7) **Group Mentoring** – *This section is intended for mentoring organizations or mentors interested in implementing a group mentoring model. It includes resources for setting up a group mentoring program, planning group mentoring lessons, and additional considerations unique to this practice.*

8) **Virtual Mentoring** – *This section is intended for mentoring organizations or mentors interested in implementing a virtual mentoring model. It includes resources for setting up a virtual mentoring program, planning virtual mentoring lessons, and additional considerations unique to this practice.*

As you read through the curriculum, you will notice that certain activities have been identified and coded as conducive to specific practices:

> Activities that apply components of Social-Emotional Learning are marked SEL.
>
> Activities that can be used in Group Mentoring are marked GM.
>
> Activities that can be used in Virtual Mentoring are marked VM.

ACTIVITIES 1-17

When mentors and mentees share their interests, values, and personal experiences, they begin to forge a bond of mutual trust and respect. Your goal as a mentor is to guide, support, and empower your mentee as they begin to understand how their goals, interests, values, and experiences affect their future academic success. In this section, "Getting to Know You," the activities are divided into three categories:

Exploring Personal Interests, Activities 1-5.

These activities will enable you to learn more about your mentee by helping them identify their interests, their opinions on a wide range of topics, and their likes and dislikes. As you complete these activities, you will have many opportunities to share your own experiences and opinions with your mentee.

Setting Realistic Goals, Activities 6-9.

This group of activities is intended to enable your mentee to establish realistic short- and long-term goals. It is very easy for adolescents to set long-term goals, but too often they lose sight of the fact that achieving short-term goals is a crucial step toward attaining the long-term ones.

Building Positive Values, Activities 10-17.

This set of activities is designed to focus your mentee's attention on the positive values that will guide them toward success and happiness in life. Young people need to learn the basic principles of personal and social responsibility, the tactics of emotional control, and the importance of personal integrity to ensure greater success in school and in adult life.

Resource List:

The following websites may help you continue to explore personal interests and values with your mentee:

- www.viacharacter.org – Offers a free character-strengths evaluation

- www.lifevaluesInventory.org – Offers an inventory assessment that identifies the mentee's values and provides tools to explore careers and educational majors aligned with each value (financial prosperity, concern for others, independence, etc.)

- www.actforyouth.net/youth_development/professionals/sel/ – A website dedicated to youth empowerment, offering tools and resources for building mentee competency in the five components of social-emotional learning — self-awareness, self-management, social awareness, relationship skills, and responsible decision-making

GETTING TO KNOW YOU

Exploring Personal Interests
Activity 1: Hot Topics

Appropriate For: SEL, GM

Learning Objective:
The mentee will engage in a meaningful conversation with an adult.

Materials Needed:
Copy of "Hot Topics" worksheet, scissors, hat or basket.

Instructions:
Select a comfortable place where you and your mentee can engage in conversation. Cut the conversation topics below into squares. Then fold each individual square so that the conversation topic cannot be seen. Alternating turns with your mentee, select one folded square at a time, read the topic, and share your response. Remember to encourage your mentee to express their opinions. Let them know that there is no wrong answer! From the responses, you will learn much more about your mentee and they will appreciate knowing that an adult cares enough to ask their opinion. This activity is easily adaptable to the group setting as well — just have mentees alternate selecting a topic and then share their response with the group.

Pay attention to which thoughts and opinions you and your mentee share in common. Try to remember what your thoughts on these topics might have been at their age and always remember to keep an open mind!

Hot Topics

If you could be the **best in the world** at something, what would you pick? Why?	Is it better to be a **morning** person or a **night** person?	What **activity** have you always wanted to try but never had the opportunity?	Is it better to be the **oldest** or **youngest** member of your family?
If your friends had to describe you in **three words**, what would they be?	If you could **travel** anywhere in the world, where would you go? Why?	If you won a million dollars tomorrow, what is the first thing you would do?	Describe your **hero**. What qualities do you admire most about this person?
Which **three items** would you take with you to a desert island?	Which **color** best describes your personality? Why?	What is the best **tradition** at your school? Why?	What three things are you most **grateful** for?
If you could meet any **famous person**, whom would you pick and why?	What is the best **book** you've ever read? Why would you recommend it?	If you could choose your own **superpower**, what you would pick?	Describe your **dream job** as a teenager? As an adult?
What **emoji** do you use most? Why?	If you were granted three **wishes**, what would they be?	Would you rather travel **back in time** or forward into the **future**? Why?	Would you vote for **year-round school**? Why or why not?
If you had to **give up** your phone, your music, or the internet, what would you give up?	Would you rather go to a **co-ed** or single-sex school? Why?	If you could **rid the world** of one thing, what would it be?	If you were **invisible** for one day, what would you do?

GETTING TO KNOW YOU

Exploring Personal Interests
Activity 2: A Few of My Favorite Things

Appropriate For: SEL, VM

Learning Objective:
The mentee and mentor will build trust and identify commonalities by sharing their personal preferences.

Materials Needed:
Copies of "A Few of My Favorite Things" worksheet, pen/pencil.

Instructions:
Prior to beginning the session, provide your mentee with a copy of this worksheet. Ask the mentee to take ten minutes to write their responses to each "favorite." You should plan to do the same. During your session, compare notes. How are your responses similar? Where do they differ? As you compare, try to identify at least a few commonalities. When possible, ask your mentee to provide further context to their response (e.g., "Why do you like X?").

Finding common ground will help strengthen your relationship with your mentee. Based on the preferences and similarities identified, work together to plan out the perfect shared day: Where would you go? What activities would you take part in? What food would you eat? What music would you listen to? What season would it be?

A Few of My Favorite Things	
Book	
Song	
Movie	
TV Show	
Color	
Season	
Celebrity	
Place to Be	
Hobby	
Food	
Website	
Sport or Game	
Author	
Holiday	
Day of the Week	
School Subject	
Animal	
Memory	
Emoji	
Family Tradition	
Teacher	

GETTING TO KNOW YOU

Exploring Personal Interests
Activity 3: What Makes Me Tick

Appropriate For: SEL, VM, GM

Learning Objective:
The mentee will explore their personal values, interests, and experiences and share their insight with their mentor.

Materials Needed:
None.

Instructions: Read the phrases aloud and ask your mentee to orally complete them with the first idea that comes to mind.

- If I had a week-long vacation, I would ...
- On weekends, I wish my family would ...
- If I had $10, I would ...
- I think my parents should ...
- The thing that scares me the most is ...
- People I like always ...
- I cry when ...
- I am afraid to ...
- I am happy when ...
- I am proud that I ...
- When I grow up, I want to be ...
- The most important quality in a family is ...
- I like people who ...
- Five years from now, I would like to ...
- I would like to travel to ...
- I would like to make a difference in the world by ...
- I am really good at ...
- I get angry when ...
- My friends think I am ...
- I am loneliest when ...
- In school, I do my best when ...
- I feel the most loved when ...

Choose a response to a phrase discussed above that caught your attention, and encourage your mentee to elaborate on their answer. Share your answers as well, identifying scenarios where you have felt similar or had similar experiences and how you chose to handle it.

GETTING TO KNOW YOU

Exploring Personal Interests
Activity 4: Highs and Lows

Appropriate For: SEL, GM

Learning Objective:
The mentee will use listening and speaking strategies to communicate effectively.

Materials:
Copy of "Highs and Lows" worksheet, scissors, pen/pencil.

Instructions:
What does your mentee consider "success" and "failure"? What things do they fear the most? These questions are important because they allow you to see things from your mentee's perspective. Cut the phrases below into squares. Then fold each individual square so that the phrase cannot be seen. Have your mentee select one folded square at a time, read the phrase, and discuss their response. Encourage your mentee to focus on accentuating the positive aspects of each answer: Was there a silver lining? An important lesson learned? This activity is easily adaptable to a group setting.

As you discuss, help your mentee recognize their unique strengths and skills, such as courage, compassion, or empathy. They might not appreciate how their unique characteristics contributed to their successes.

Highs and Lows

My greatest success in life is....	My greatest academic achievement is....
I am proud of....	A situation or experience I wish I could "do over" is....
I most fear....	I would most like to learn....
Something I did that took courage was....	Something I wish I was better at is....
A lesson I learned from a mistake was....	One thing that is hard for me is....

GETTING TO KNOW YOU

Exploring Personal Interests
Activity 5: More About Me

Appropriate For: SEL, GM, VM

Learning Objective:
The mentee will discover their personality type.

Materials Needed:
Internet access.

Instructions:
Select one of the following websites, all of which offer free personality assessments:

- **www.123test.com/personality-test/** – Personality assessment based on the Big Five personality framework
- **www.humanmetrics.com/cgi-win/jtypes2.asp** – Personality assessment based on the Myers-Briggs framework
- **www.16personalities.com/free-personality-test** – Personality assessment based on the Neris framework
- **www.you.visualdna.com/quiz/whoami#/quiz** – Unique personality assessment that uses visuals to assess your type

You and your mentee should both take the test you select, prior to your session. If possible, read the descriptions of the personality types according to the correlating framework before taking the test. See if you can each guess your personality type before completing the assessment. At the session, share your personality type. What are the strengths for this personality type? What are the challenges? Then decide if you think each of your results were accurate – was the type correct? Or are you/your mentee a mix of several types? Based on what you decide, what are the academic areas of interest or career pathways that might align best with your mentee's type? This may offer some insight into pathways he or she has never considered before.

GETTING TO KNOW YOU

Setting Realistic Goals
Activity 6: S.M.A.R.T. Goals

Appropriate For: SEL, GM, VM

Learning Objective:
The mentee will gain an understanding of the effective process for setting and measuring personal goals.

Materials Needed:
Copy of "S.M.A.R.T. Goals" worksheet, pen/pencil, sentence strips or student journal.

Instructions:
Review the content below with your mentee. Work together to craft a S.M.A.R.T. goal for your mentoring pair (or group). Then have your mentee work on setting their own S.M.A.R.T. goals and recording them on sentence strips or in a journal.

S.M.A.R.T. GOALS

Goals: what you would like to achieve

Objectives: how you will reach your goals

Specific

Consider writing a goal that is specific, clearly defines what you want, and answers the Who? What? Where? When? and Why? to achieve it.

Measurable

Establish concrete criteria for measuring your success and progress. To determine if measurable, ask questions like, "How much?" "How many?" and "How will I know when reach I my goal?"

Achievable

Create a realistic path to achievement that includes action steps and objectives. Your goals should push you past your comfort point; however, you should be able to attain them with dedication and commitment.

Relevant

Consider what the purpose of achieving your goal is. Your goals should be important to you, and the outcome should have positive impact on your life.

Timely

Use actual numbers, target dates, or specific events to indicate when your goal will be achieved.

Sample S.M.A.R.T. Goal:

I, John Smith, will begin attending XYZ College in Fall 2019. I will begin coursework to achieve a Bachelor's Degree in Criminal Justice by Spring 2024.

Sample Objectives:

- I will attend all five sessions of my school's SAT prep course.
- I will work with my mentor and parents to complete the FAFSA form by April 1, 2019.
- I will get at least a B in my AP Government class and will sign up for AP American History next term.

GETTING TO KNOW YOU

Setting Realistic Goals
Activity 7: I Have S.M.A.R.T. Goals

Appropriate For: SEL, VM

Learning Objective:
The mentee will create goals for different aspects of their lives.

Materials Needed:
Copies of "I Have S.M.A.R.T. Goals" worksheet, pencil or pen.

Instructions
Use the worksheet below to talk through a sample goal in one aspect of your own life (academic, career, or personal). Then work together to craft a goal for your mentee's life, letting them choose the achievement they would like to work on. Discuss a plan to periodically check in with each other on your goals. If one goal is completed, use this format to create an action plan for achieving another!

I Have S.M.A.R.T. Goals

My Goal: _____

_____

_____

Type of Goal (check one): Academic _____ Career _____ Personal _____

Specific (Who, What, When): _____

_____

_____

Measurable (How much/many): _____

_____

_____

Achievable (Steps I'll take): _____

_____

_____

Relevant (Important because): _____

_____

_____

Timely (I will achieve by): _____

_____

_____

Setting Realistic Goals
Activity 8: My Vision Board

Appropriate For: SEL, GM

Learning Objective:
The mentee will create and share a visual illustration of their short- and long-term goals.

Materials:
Copies of "My Vision Board" worksheet; poster board (one per mentee if using in a group setting), a variety of old magazines, glue, scissors, markers.

Instructions:
Sometimes envisioning the things you want is an effective motivator. You can use this activity to help your mentee create a "Vision Board." Ask your mentee to cut out pictures from old magazines that represent what they want to achieve in their future. Their pictures could represent a range of goals, including professional, academic, and personal. Then provide your mentee with poster board to create a collage of their vision.

To encourage discussion, ask your mentee to use the space provided to list the pictures they chose and briefly explain why they chose to include several in their collage. When the collages are finished, have them share their poster. Mentors are encouraged to make one as well to share! This activity is easily adaptable to the group setting – encourage mentees to share their vision with their peers!

My Vision Board

PICTURE	EXPLANATION

GETTING TO KNOW YOU

Setting Realistic Goals
Activity 9: Looking Through the Crystal Ball

Appropriate For: SEL

Learning Objective:
The mentee will think about long-term life goals.

Materials Needed:
Copies of "Looking Through the Crystal Ball" worksheet, pen/pencil.

Instructions:
Mentees who have concrete goals in life are more likely to be motivated to succeed. Encourage your mentee to complete this worksheet while you do the same. Ask questions to guide your mentee to think practically and realistically. Remember to acknowledge the value of your mentee's answers. Encourage them to dream big!

Looking Through the Crystal Ball

Family Life You Would Like to Have:	Place You Would Like to Live:
One Year:	One Year:
Five Years:	Five Years:
Ten Years:	Ten Years:

Topics You Want to Learn About:	Career Path You Would Like Be On:
One Year:	One Year:
Five Years:	Five Years:
Ten Years:	Ten Years:

Places You Would Like to Visit:	People You Would Like to Be Like:
One Year:	One Year
Five Years:	Five Years:
Ten Years:	Ten Years:

Skills You Would Like to Develop:	Interests You Would Like to Develop:
One Year:	One Year:
Five Years:	Five Years:
Ten Years:	Ten Years:

GETTING TO KNOW YOU

Building Positive Values
Activity 10: I'm Positively Charged

Appropriate For: SEL, VM

Learning Objective:
The mentee will develop a positive attitude towards dealing with emotions.

Materials Needed:
Copy of "I'm Positively Charged" worksheet, pen/pencil.

Instructions:
Ask your mentee to complete the following sentences. Share your responses as well to signal that all answers are okay and no one is perfect! Getting young people to reflect on the relationship between their behavior and their feelings is an important step in their personal growth.

Remind your mentee that, while they may not be able to control the way people treat them, they can control the way they react in a situation. They should try to remain positive and constructive when dealing with difficult moments. Together with your mentee, identify which reactions could be replaced with a more positive approach and what those action steps might look like. Record these actions in the space at the bottom of the page.

I'm Positively Charged

When I cannot have my own way, I...

When I fail at something, I...

When I am nervous, I...

When I am punished, I...

When I get angry with my teacher, I...

When I cannot go out with my friends, I...

When my friends make me mad, I...

When I am picked on by others, I...

When I am bored, I...

When I am embarrassed, I...

Action Plan:

_____

_____

_____

GETTING TO KNOW YOU

Building Positive Values
Activity 11: What's Going Well

Appropriate For: SEL, VM, GM

Learning Objective:
The mentee will reflect on the week's activities and gain insight and practice on observing and identifying positive experiences.

Materials:
Copies of "What's Going Well" worksheet, pencils/pens.

Instructions:
Start by giving your mentee several minutes to complete the "What's Going Well" worksheet. You should complete it as well. Then go back and forth with each response sharing your answers. As often as possible, work with your mentee to highlight the positive side or lesson in at least one challenging situation identified. As appropriate, make an action plan for any component of the week that did not go well (see Activities 6-7 on setting SMART goals).

If using in a group setting, start by putting mentees into pairs and asking them to share their responses with each other. When one partner is sharing, the other person should listen carefully and respond back with the positive experiences they heard reflected. Time permitting, allow mentees to share their reflections with the group as well

What's Going Well?	27
What was the high point of the week?	
Did you get to know anyone a little better this week?	
Did you make any major (or even minor!) changes in your life this week?	
Did you accomplish any goals this week?	
Did you help anyone this week? Or did anyone help you?	
What decisions/choices did you make this week?	
Did you make any plans for future events this week?	
What are you most looking forward to next week?	

GETTING TO KNOW YOU

Building Positive Values
Activity 12: Tap into Positive Emotions

Appropriate For: SEL, GM

Learning Objective:
The mentee will create an illustration to refocus on goals and positive emotions when they're feeling discouraged.

Materials Needed:
Copy of "Tap into Positive Emotions" worksheet, old magazines, scissors, glue stick, poster board (one per mentee if using in a group setting), markers.

Instructions:
Tapping into a positive emotion can also be a source of strength. Choose one positive emotion your mentee would like to experience more of and list the pictures that help them tap into that emotion. Work together to create a poster that will remind them of their goals when they have a bad day. You can also spend time brainstorming other creative ways to tap into positive emotions. For example, mentees could change the background picture on their phone to something that helps them think positively or put a picture in their locker that inspires them.

Tap into Positive Emotions

Positive Emotions

Joy	**Pride**
Gratitude	**Amusement**
Serenity	**Inspiration**
Interest	**Awe**
Hope	**Love**

When _____

I feel _____

Images that remind me of this feeling include:

_____   _____

_____   _____

_____   _____

_____   _____

GETTING TO KNOW YOU

Building Positive Values
Activity 13: Responsibility = Success

Appropriate For: SEL, VM

Learning Objective:
The mentee will understand the relationship between responsibility and success.

Materials Needed:
Copy of "Responsibility=Success" worksheet, pen/pencil.

Instructions:
This exercise is an easy way to guide your mentee into realizing that being responsible is the key to being successful. Encourage your mentee to answer the questions by placing a mark in either column A or B below. Be sure to share what you struggled with most as a student – it is important that your mentee feels they can share their challenges without feeling judged. Then work with your mentee to complete column C. This is an opportunity to discuss how developing responsible behavior in simple daily tasks leads to success.

Responsibility = Success

Do you...	A Yes	B Needs Improvement	C To be more successful, I can....
Get to school on time?			
Come to class prepared?			
Take complete notes during class?			
Study for tests?			
Complete all assignments?			
Do extra credit assignments?			
Pay attention in class?			
Turn in your homework?			
Get good grades?			
Put forth 100% effort in all classes?			

GETTING TO KNOW YOU

Building Positive Values
Activity 14: Because I'm Worth It

Appropriate For: SEL, GM

Learning Objective:
The mentee will engage in meaningful conversation with an adult.

Materials Needed:
Copy of "Because I'm Worth It" worksheet, pen/pencil.

Instructions:
It is important for mentees to feel that they are valued and respected. This is why building their self-esteem is so important. Help your mentee build their self-esteem by encouraging them to complete the following six steps. Then ask your mentee which of the steps was the most difficult to answer and why. This activity can also be done in pairs for a group setting.

Because I'm Worth It

Step 1: Think of the qualities that make you unique.
What are your strengths and unique talents?

_____

_____

_____

Step 2: Be responsible for yourself and your decisions.
What are three decisions you need to make on your own?

1. _____

2. _____

3. _____

Step 3: Recognize mistakes as stepping–stones to success.
List a mistake that helped you learn or improve.

_____

_____

_____

Step 4: Show friends you have an interest in them.
List three things you can do to show people you care about them.

1. _____

2. _____

3. _____

Step 5: Think things through.
Make a list of three things you want most to learn or improve.

1. _____

2. _____

3. _____

Step 6: Get involved in activities you like.
List extracurricular activities, volunteer opportunities, or hobbies that interest you.

_____

_____

_____

GETTING TO KNOW YOU

Building Positive Values
Activity 15: Cross Out Bullying

Appropriate For: SEL, GM, VM

Learning Objective:
The mentee will build their vocabulary on bullying.

Materials Needed:
Copies of "Cross Out Bullying" crossword puzzle, pen/pencil.

Instructions:
Work together with your mentee to complete the crossword puzzle below on bullying terms. As you work, discuss what each of the terms means and how it might apply to real-life scenarios your mentee could encounter.

CROSS OUT BULLYING CROSSWORD

Word Bank

Empathy	Victim	Ethics
Bully	Relentless	Ridicule
Intervene	Taunt	
Alternative	Influence	

ACROSS

1. To come between; solve a problem; speak for another; prevent an incident from happening.

4. To reproach with insulting words.

6. Person, or thing, destroyed or sacrificed; person who suffers.

7. Overbearing person who tyrannizes the weak.

8. To have capacity to affect others' behaviors and opinions.

9. Offering a choice of two things; selecting a course of action.

10. Relating to morals or moral principles; philosophy of human character and conduct; of distinction between right and wrong; rules of conduct.

DOWN

2. Intellectual identification of oneself with another; understanding the attitudes of others.

3. Mocking; to make fun of; speech or action intended to cause contemptuous laughter at another person.

5. Unyieldingly severe, mean, or harsh

GETTING TO KNOW YOU

Building Positive Values
Activity 16: What Would You Do?

Appropriate For: SEL, GM, VM

Learning Objective:
The mentee will gain a basic understanding of bullying.

Materials Needed:
None

Instructions:
Equipping mentees with the tools they need to feel safe in school will provide a better learning environment for them. Discuss possible solutions to the scenarios below with your mentee. This can be done in pairs, with a group share-out as well. Remember to keep an open mind when listening to your mentee's responses – these scenarios can be very tricky for adolescents to navigate.

- Jessica always sits alone at lunch; others sometimes throw things at her. You've talked to her a few times and know she is very shy but nice. However, you know if you sit with her, your friends will tease you.
- Juan is punched by another student at his locker every day. Your locker is next to his, so you witness this daily and it bothers you, but you aren't sure what to do about it.
- You just heard of a plan for a big fight on the bus. Your friends are all planning to go to watch and want you to go with them.
- Maria wrote a song with mean lyrics about another girl; she shares it with you and tells you to pass it on. You know it will make your friends laugh, but you aren't sure if you should.
- Someone posted something mean or untrue about you on a social media platform that lots of students at your school use.

For more information and activities on bullying, check out the following websites:

www.discoveryeducation.com/teachers/free-lesson-plans/cruel-schools.cfm
Discover solutions to managing anger, getting help, and stopping violence.

www.bullyingstatistics.org
Information on preventing bullying, harassment, violence, online bullying, and school bullies.

www.pacer.org/bullying/classroom/
Provides lesson plans and toolkits for talking to students about bullying.

GETTING TO KNOW YOU

Building Positive Values
Activity 17: Tick-Tock on the Clock

Appropriate For: SEL, VM

Learning Objective:
The mentee will develop time management skills.

Materials Needed:
Copies of "Tick-Tock on the Clock" worksheet, calendar or planner, pen/pencil.

Instructions:
Developing good time management skills will help your mentee throughout their entire lives, from secondary school to post-secondary to the workforce. Help your mentee identify time management issues they may have and help them to brainstorm workable solutions.

Tick-Tock on the Clock

When working on time management, it is important to consider the following:

- Consider everything you HAVE to do and WANT to do.
- When planning your time, make sure to identify the most important things first, working your way down to things that can wait a couple of days or weeks.
- Estimate as accurately as possible how much time each activity will take, always leaving a little extra.
- Using a calendar, make a plan that helps you navigate the day, week, and month.

Complete the phrases below. This will help you identify areas of improvement:

- The most important priorities for my time are:
- I feel I spend too much of my time on:
- I feel like I do not have enough time for:
- I feel I spend **too much**, **not enough**, **just enough** (circle one) time on homework. Here are some ways I could better manage my homework time:
- I feel I spend **too much**, **not enough**, **just enough** (circle one) time on extracurricular activities and sports.
- Here are some ways I could better manage my activity time:
- I feel I spend **too much**, **not enough**, **just enough** (circle one) time on self-care (sleep, healthy eating, exercise).
- Here are some ways I could take better care of my health:
- One sport, club, or activity I would not want to do without is_____ because:
- My favorite way to spend free time is:
- The most effective way to relieve stress for me is:

Action Plan:

_____

_____

_____

_____

_____

SECTION ② SOCIAL–EMOTIONAL LEARNING

Introduction

Social-emotional learning (SEL) is the process through which individuals obtain the knowledge and skills necessary to recognize and manage their own emotions, build and maintain relationships, and appropriately and productively respond to emotions in others. Although recognition of the value of SEL to the healthy development of children and adolescents is a relatively recent phenomenon, the education field is increasingly aware of the critical importance of students learning these skills in order to succeed in post-secondary education and career. You may hear of these skills referred to by other names: Essential Life Skills, Executive Functioning, 21st Century Skills, etc. No matter how you refer to them, the research is clear: social-emotional skills are a critical component to personal success and happiness – in school, in the workplace, and in life.

As a mentor, you are uniquely situated to provide your mentees with the guidance, support, and role-modeling needed to develop their social-emotional capacity, particularly for mentees who aren't receiving it in their school or home setting. Furthermore, SEL is well-aligned to most typical mentoring goals, and may even be helpful in achieving them. Research has shown that explicit social-emotional instruction for students can result in improved classroom behaviors, an increased ability to manage stress, and a more positive opinion of themselves, their peers, and their school.

Fortunately, the mentoring process naturally creates consistent opportunities for mentees to observe, internalize, and practice their effective social skills with a thoughtful and caring adult. To help you further incorporate social-emotional learning into your mentoring planning, we've included a range of activities that address the five key competencies of SEL:

- **Self-Awareness** – *Recognizing one's own emotions, values, personal strengths, and challenges*
- **Self-Management** – *Managing emotions and behaviors to achieve personal goals*
- **Social Awareness** – *Understanding and appropriately responding to the needs of others*
- **Relationship Skills** – *Forming healthy, respectful connections with others*
- **Responsible Decision-Making** – *Making decisions that best support both short-term and long-term life goals*

To find the exercises in this toolkit that will help mentees build the 5 Competencies of Social-Emotional Learning, look for the code **SEL**. We have also included 5 additional exercises designed specifically to help develop your mentee's social-emotional skills.

SOCIAL-EMOTIONAL LEARNING

Activity 18: The One Minute Reflection

Appropriate For: SEL

Learning Objective:
The mentee and mentor will practice the social emotional skill of self-awareness.

Materials Needed:
Paper, pencils.

Instructions:
This activity can be used to start off any mentoring session.

Choose one of the prompts below. Using a timer, give your mentee 60 seconds to write (or draw) as many responses to the prompt as possible. At the end, have them choose one response to discuss in greater detail. You can also identify one you would like to discuss further.

Prompts:

- What did you accomplish this day/week?
- What do you like most about yourself?
- What are you good at?
- What emotions did you experience this week?
- What strategies would help resolve a problem you had this week (a bad grade on a test, a fight with a friend)?
- How have you taken care of your health/wellness this week?
- What made you happy this week?
- What made you sad this week?
- What makes you angry?
- What are you most excited about for the future?
- What are you most proud of?
- What were the highs and lows of the past week?
- What did you do this week/month to reach X goal?

SOCIAL-EMOTIONAL LEARNING

Activity 19: Get in the Zone!

Appropriate For: SEL

Learning Objective:
The mentee and mentor will practice the social emotional skill of self-management.

Materials Needed:
Zones of Regulation Worksheet

Instructions:
The Zones of Regulation is a framework used to teach self-regulation and management. The worksheet below could be used with your mentee at the beginning of every session as an initial check-in; it could also be used as an intervention when your mentee comes into a session feeling a particularly intense emotion (anger, sadness, excitement, etc.). Note: it may be advisable to practice some of the Zone interventions - such as deep breathing - at a session where your mentee is calm, so the skill is already familiar when needed.

1. Look at the Zones of Regulation worksheet. Decide together which color most resonates with how your mentee is feeling in the moment.

2. If Green, proceed with the session as planned. If Yellow, Blue, or Red, choose one of the interventions to use. Sometimes it may be necessary to do more than one intervention before your mentee feels ready to discuss how they are feeling – for example, if they identify they are in the 'Blue' zone, you may offer them a snack and give them ten minutes to write in a journal, before attempting to talk.

3. Once your mentee feels ready, discuss how they are feeling and why. The following questions may be helpful in framing the discussion:

   • What zone were you in before the intervention(s)?
   • What zone are you in now?
   • What is causing the intense feeling? Is there a specific issue or problem? Multiple issues?
   • How does the problem or issue feel now that you are calm? Has it grown "smaller"?
   • What action steps can be taken to remedy the issue in the short run? In the long run?

Zones of Regulation

Sometimes when we are feeling strong emotions, it can be difficult to determine exactly what we are feeling or why – we only know that we feel "off". The zones of regulation are a way to help us identify how we are feeling in a particular moment, as well as select the appropriate interventions to help us through an upsetting or confusing situation. The zones were originally developed for use with elementary students, but can be a really helpful resource for individuals of any age!

There are four zones. They are:

Zone 1: Green	**Zone 2: Blue**
Definition: Feeling in control.	Definition: Feeling low levels of alertness.
Associated emotions: happy, calm, focused, content.	Associated emotions: sad, tired, sick, bored.
Ideal for: completing tasks (such as schoolwork), taking tests, being social with friends.	Interventions: rest, talking with a trusted friend or mentor, gentle exercise, eating a healthy snack that includes protein, journaling.
Zone 3: Yellow	**Zone 4: Red**
Definition: Emotions are heightened, starting to feel out of control. Could go back down to Zone 1 or up to Zone 4, depending how the situation is handled.	Definition: Emotions are very intense. Feeling very out of control.
Associated emotions: excitement, mild stress or anxiety, frustration.	Associated emotions: anger, rage, panic, fear.
Interventions: Deep breathing, gentle exercise (such as a walk outside), talking with a trusted friend or mentor.	Interventions: more intense exercise (a quick jog, lifting weights, wall pushups, punch a punching bag), meditation activity (sitting in a comfortable spot and taking ten deep breaths).

SOCIAL-EMOTIONAL LEARNING

Activity 20: Active Listening 101

Appropriate For: SEL

Learning Objective:
The mentee and mentor will practice the social-emotional skill of social awareness.

Materials Needed:
Active Listening Worksheet

Instructions:
The abilities to show empathy and listen effectively are two of the most crucial components of emotional intelligence. Furthermore, research shows that employers increasingly value these skills in the workplace, even more than technical skills or content knowledge. Active listening strategies are one way to practice developing these capacities.

1. With your mentee, review the Active Listening worksheet.
2. Choose one of the following prompts.
3. Set a timer for one minute. While your mentee responds to the prompt, model the active listening strategies listed on the sheet.
4. When the timer goes off, take a minute to reflect on the experience. What part of active listening was easiest to implement? Which was the most challenging?
5. Set the timer again – this time you will respond to the prompt, while your mentee actively listens.
6. Repeat the self-reflection step – ask your mentee how the experience felt. What part of active listening was easiest for them? Most challenging?

Active Listening

Active listening is a method of listening to another person speak, that allows that individual to feel heard and understood. It is called active listening because it requires particular actions on the part of the listener; although you not speaking, your role is active rather than passive!

When implementing active listening, use the following strategies:

1. Listen without interrupting – wait until the person is finished to ask a question or clarification. This can be harder than it seems to actually do!
2. Make eye contact – ensure your eyes stay on the speaker the entire time they are talking.
3. Smile – Nonverbally encourage the speaker to complete their thought but smiling while they speak.
4. Maintain welcoming body language – Your body should be turned towards the speaker. Your hands and feet should be still throughout the experience.
5. Summarize – When the speaker is finished, summarize back what you heard them say, using an "I" statement, such as "I hear you saying…." or "I understand you feel _____ because…."
6. Ask questions or for clarifications – Show that you care enough to fully understand the other person's viewpoint by asking clarifying questions about the information shared.

SOCIAL EMOTIONAL LEARNING

Activity 21: Shared Goals

Appropriate For: SEL

Learning Objective:
The mentee and mentor will practice the social emotional skill of relationship-building.

Materials Needed:
Shared Goal Worksheet

Instructions:
Part of relationship-building is learning to work collaboratively with others – a skill that is essential for success in school and the workplace. With your mentee, discuss and select a goal that you will work towards together. Then, using the Shared Goal worksheet, collectively develop a plan for how you will complete the goal.

Some Ideas for Shared Mentor/Mentee Goals:

- Walk/run/swim/bike _____ miles (or steps) by the end of the school year
- Read and hold weekly discussions on a challenging book
- Learn and practice a new skill you are both interested in
- Complete an online course together
- Fundraise a set amount of money for a cause you both feel strongly about (or Commit to volunteering a set number of hours by the end of the year)
- Make a joint list of activities you've always wanted to try but have been too afraid to attempt – and complete it!
- Create your own!

Shared Goals

Goal:

Timeline for Completing:

To Complete This Goal, We Will:

1.

2.

3.

4.

5.

We will measure our progress by:

SOCIAL-EMOTIONAL LEARNING

Activity 22: How Do I Decide?

Appropriate For: SEL

Learning Objective:
The mentee and mentor will practice the social emotional skill of responsible decision-making.

Materials Needed:
How Do I Decide? worksheet

Instructions:
This activity can be used any time your mentee is struggling to make an important decision. You can also use this worksheet to practice making decisions using made-up scenarios.

Example Scenario:

You just received acceptance letters to two colleges. The first college is your dream school – the school you have always wanted to attend – and you are thrilled to get in. The school is known for having a great department for the major you are interested in. Your favorite teacher went there as well, and you know she would be so proud to have you go there. However, the school is very expensive and attending will require you to work part-time while in school and possibly take loans as well. It is also much farther away from home than you originally wanted to go.

The second college seemed nice when you visited. The campus is pretty and located much closer to home. It is also much less expensive the first. Between scholarships and money you have saved, you would not need to take a loan to attend. However, you are not as excited about attending. It is a much bigger school than you saw yourself going to. While it does offer your major, the program isn't well-known as it is at your dream school.

Which college should you choose?

How Do I Decide?

Describe the Problem:

Possible Solutions

Option A:	Option C:
Option B:	Option D:

Possible Outcomes (Short-term and Long-term)

For Option A	For Option C
For Option B	For Option D

Values I Hold that Impact This Decision:

People Impacted by This Decision:

The Best Decision for Me:

Activities 23 – 31
Supporting Academic Success

The activities in this section will allow you to learn how to provide support for your mentee in specific subject areas and empower you to encourage your mentee in developing important organizational and academic skills. The goal is to assist your mentee in higher scholastic achievement through the use of proven strategies and techniques.

Improving Academic Skills, Activities 23-31

These activities are designed to introduce your mentee to the basic organizational skills necessary for academic success. Colleges report that two of the main causes of poor academic performance among freshmen are inadequate organizational ability and lack of self-discipline. These activities are designed to target these basic skills, to both improve current academic performance and prepare students for the post-secondary experience.

Resource List:

The following websites may help you continue to explore academic skills with your mentee:

- **www.khanacademy.com** Learn for free about math, art, computer programming, economics, physics, chemistry, biology, medicine, finance, history, and more.
- **www.educationcorner.com/study-skills.html** Provides resources for developing stronger study skills.
- **www.powa.org** Instructional site for students who need support to improve their writing skills.
- **www.howtostudy.org** Offers resources for studying, organized by academic subject.

SUPPORTING ACADEMIC SUCCESS

Improving Academic Skills
Activity 23: Identifying and Addressing Your Mentee's Needs

Materials Needed: None.

Instructions: If allowed by your mentoring organization, you can get a fairly clear picture of your mentee's school performance by reviewing their progress reports and report cards, both present and past. These reports will include information such as absences, tardies, suspensions, grades, and academic effort, all of which can help you identify where your mentee may need the most support. Reports may also include specific comments and recommendations made by your mentee's previous teachers. Below are some recommendations to help you identify and address your mentee's specific academic needs.

Obtain your mentee's progress report and/or report card.

Compare academic progress from one grading period to the next. Look for trends in achievement, attendance, and conduct. As you look over the report, ask yourself a few questions: Is there a problem with attendance or conduct? Is your mentee always prepared for class? Is adequate progress being made? Are my mentee's grades reflective of their best efforts? If there are areas where improvement is needed, address these with your mentee. It is most productive to allow your mentee to self-identify their challenges and then spend some time brainstorming potential strategies or resources that might help. If your mentee doesn't identify an obvious challenge noted in their reports, you can gently bring it up, with a goal of identifying the root of the issue to see if it can be addressed – a non-judgmental tone is key. As always, it may be helpful to discuss your own academic challenges with your mentee as a means of developing trust.

Pay close attention to your mentee's grades on an ongoing basis.

Grades are the key performance indicators for your mentee. Waiting until the report card is released may allow too much time to elapse before a problem is identified and addressed. Remind your mentee that it is important for them to perform their academic best, in order to succeed in applying to post-secondary programming. You might consider starting every session by asking what their academic successes and challenges were for the week so you can celebrate the wins and brainstorm action steps to help with issues as they arise.

Incorporate Academics into Your Session as Appropriate.

If your mentee is struggling – or is especially interested – in a particular area or subject, see if there are ways you could provide further support or help develop their interest. For example, if your mentee is writing a paper on a certain topic, send them a current article related to the content that you could discuss at your next session, or use an online platform to collaboratively explore a relevant website. If your organization allows it, you might consider taking your mentee on a fieldtrip or to see a film that relates to what they are studying. You could also help provide editing or other forms of feedback to written assignments.

SUPPORTING ACADEMIC SUCCESS

Improving Academic Skills
Activity 24: What Works for Me

Appropriate For: VM

Learning Objective:
The mentee will identify the academic strategies that work best for them.

Materials Needed:
Internet access.

Instructions:
Students learn in a variety of different ways, and everyone has different strategies and techniques that will work best for their personality and preferences. Go to one (or more) of the links below, and review the suggestions and habits identified with your mentee.

- https://oedb.org/ilibrarian/hacking-knowledge/
- https://www.goconqr.com/en/examtime/blog/good-habits-for-students/
- https://vlacs.org/top-10-study-tips-students/
- https://thinkeracademy.com/21-study-tips/

Once you and your mentee have reviewed at least one of these lists, discuss the following questions:

- Based on the suggestions given, what are some new ideas you could incorporate into your study habits?
- Which habits are most appealing?
- Which habits do you already have but could improve upon?
- What (if any) resources or supports do you need to incorporate each of these habits into your life?

It may be helpful to create specific SMART goals around each of the habits your mentee would like to work on, as well as a timeline for when to check in regarding progress. (For more on setting SMART Goals, see Activities 6 & 7 in this toolkit).

SUPPORTING ACADEMIC SUCCESS

Improving Academic Skills
Activity 25: Time Management 101

Appropriate For: SEL, GM

Learning Objective:
The mentee will learn how to utilize their planner to facilitate academic success through efficient time management.

Materials Needed:
Copy of "Time Management 101" worksheet, pen/pencil, your personal planner. Mentee(s) should also bring their personal planner to the session – you may need to help them obtain one if they aren't currently using one.

Instructions:
Help your mentee determine whether or not they are using their time wisely in their day-to-day activities by completing the activity below. Help them to identify the most efficient use of their time, showing them how they can input tasks and assignments and keep track of their daily schedule in their planner. Use your planner as an example. If working in a group setting, you may want to pair mentees up, and have them provide each other feedback with how well they are currently using their planners.

Using their answers to these questions, help your mentee identify areas where they could improve the use of their time or manage it more effectively. It may be helpful to create specific SMART goals around one or more of the areas they could work on, as well as a timeline for when to check-in regarding progress. (For more on setting SMART Goals, see Activities 6 & 7 in this toolkit.) If your mentee is not using a planner regularly, you may want to start there, to help ensure they are meeting academic deadlines and are on-track for academic success.

Time Management 101

How much time do you spend doing the following per week on...

- Studying/homework at school
- Extracurricular activities
- Family responsibilities (chores, babysitting for younger siblings, etc.)
- Study/homework at home
- Part-time job
- Volunteering
- Time with friends
- Hobbies and other interests
- Self-care (sleep, exercise, healthy meals)
- Other (be specific)

On a scale of 1-3 (1= Never; 2 = Sometimes; 3 = Always), how often do you:

- Use your planner to record your tasks and assignments?
- Review your planner at the start of the day or week to familiarize yourself with your upcoming schedule?
- Include due dates on your planner entries?
- Put tasks with the most importance at the top of your list to be completed first?
- As you complete a task, check it off so that you see your accomplishment?
- Set aside time daily or weekly to identify available spare time in your schedule?
- Use gaps in your schedule to do short, easy tasks you can complete quickly?
- Use downtime to review notes and study for upcoming tests and quizzes?
- Share your schedule with your parents?
- Give your parents the opportunity to make suggestions to accommodate your family responsibilities or provide support where needed?
- Inform your friends of your schedule so they are able to respect your time?
- Keep your coach or job supervisor informed of your weekly academic schedule so that you have the time you need to complete school assignments and study for upcoming tests?
- Schedule in time for self-care (sleep, exercise, healthy meals)?
- Make time for activities or interests you enjoy?

Action Plan:

_____

_____

_____

SUPPORTING ACADEMIC SUCCESS

Improving Academic Skills
Activity 26: The Trick to Note-Taking

Appropriate For: GM, VM

Learning Objective:
The mentee will evaluate their note-taking habits and review tips for improving this practice.

Materials Needed:
A copy of "The Trick to Note-Taking" worksheet, pen/pencil.

Instructions:
Effective note taking is important for students to retain information learned in class. Use the discussion questions below to determine whether your mentee is taking effective notes.

The Trick to Note-Taking

On a scale of 1-3 (1= Never; 2 = Sometimes; 3 = Always), how often:

- Do you review and edit your notes within 24 hours after the class where you took them?
- Do you try to write down every word your teacher says?
- Are you able to understand your notes when you study for a test?
- Do you find that you miss a lot of information when you take notes?
- Do you include drawings or sketches that help you remember the information?

Review the tips below. Which do you already use? Which could you start to incorporate?

- **Be selective**. Avoid trying to write down every word or writing in complete sentences. Key words only!
- **Abbreviate.** Reduce common words/phrases to symbols and eliminate connecting words like: is, are, was, the, and would. Drop the last few letters of words; e.g., "approx" for "approximately." Try using "formula" statements to take notes. For example, the teacher says, "The diameter of the earth is four times greater than the diameter of the moon." You write, "Earth=4x>diameter of moon."
- **Focus on the main points.** Use "significance" statements. Identify main concepts and state why they are important. If the information being given is important, a speaker will usually do one of the following: pause before or after an idea, use repetition to emphasize a point, or write an idea on the board.
- **Identify significance.** Ask yourself, is the information being discussed new or is it covered in the text? You can do this by looking over the class assignment prior to class. To be successful, make sure you are a step ahead and have a working knowledge of the topic. For information covered in the text, you only need to note key phrases you should make sure to understand.
- **Ask questions.** Make sure you clarify areas that are unclear or confusing.
- **Reference examples**. Concrete examples are often the best way to clarify complex ideas. Include drawings or other visuals as applicable.
- **Review notes ASAP.** The sooner you review your notes, the better you will retain the information.
- **Be neat**. Your notes won't do you any good if you can't read them! Each class, start your notes on a new page, with the date and title of the lecture at the top so they are easy to refer back to.
- **Leave space.** You may want to go back and add more detail when you are studying, and this will also make full pages of notes feel less overwhelming!

SUPPORTING ACADEMIC SUCCESS

Improving Academic Skills
Activity 27: My Study Habits

Appropriate For: GM, VM

Learning Objective:
The mentee will analyze their study habits and devise a plan to improve their study skills.

Materials Needed:
Copy of "My Study Habits" worksheet, pen/pencil.

Instructions:
Good study habits are a key building block to academic success. It is important for students to understand the relationship between studying and good grades.

Ask your mentee to use this questionnaire to self-assess their study habits. (For a group setting, this could be done in pairs). If your mentee answered "true" to any of these statements, work together to brainstorm practical solutions for improving their habits in this area. Discuss the importance of building strong study habits now, to maximize their academic success in high school and smooth the transition to post-secondary education. It may be helpful to start the discussion by describing your study struggles as a student, to set the expectation that everyone has areas they can improve in.

My Study Habits – Self Assessment

I never study more than an hour for tests.	true	false
I only study the night before a test.	true	false
If I study too much, I cannot have time for fun.	true	false
If I study, I do not have time for anything else.	true	false
I study with music, the television, or my phone on.	true	false
I do not have a quiet place to study	true	false
I cannot sit and study for long periods of time.	true	false
I have trouble taking notes.	true	false
I often doodle or get distracted in class.	true	false
I do not use class notes to study for tests.	true	false
I never organize my class notes.	true	false
I have trouble keeping up with my reading.	true	false
I do not always get my homework done.	true	false
I cannot recognize the main ideas in a chapter.	true	false
I would like to read faster.	true	false
I have trouble writing papers.	true	false
I do not know how to create an outline.	true	false
I put off difficult assignments until the last minute.	true	false

Action Plan:

_____

_____

_____

_____

_____

_____

_____

SUPPORTING ACADEMIC SUCCESS

Improving Academic Skills
Activity 28: Test Time!

Appropriate For: GM, VM

Learning Objective:
The mentee will become familiar with different types of test-taking strategies to use when studying.

Materials Needed:
Copies of "Test Time!" information sheet.

Instructions:
There are many different types of tests. Knowing how to study specifically for each type, whether essay, true/false, multiple choice, or a combination, can help your mentee increase their ability to score well. Review the various test preparation tips below with your mentee. Then discuss which strategies might be most useful to incorporate into their study habits. This exercise will be most effective when used in context; that is, when used to help your mentee formulate a game plan for preparing for an actual upcoming assessment. Plan to re-review these test-taking tips with your mentee prior to an upcoming test. It may be useful to practice with a few sample questions – you can find many practice quizzes in almost any topic or subject online.

Test Time!

General Test Prep Tips:

- Concentrate on learning what you do not know
- Ask your teacher for help, if necessary
- Anticipate the questions
- Make a test schedule
- Create a study outline
- Know what will be covered
- Get a good night's sleep before the test

Essay Tests

- **Keep Track of Your Time** If you have five questions to answer in 40 minutes, for example, make sure you do not spend too much time on any one question.
- **Read Through the Questions** Once By familiarizing yourself with all the questions first, you will have much more time to consider your answers.
- **Identify the Directive Words** Read the directions carefully and pinpoint the key terms. If a teacher wants you to describe, then do so; if she wants you to evaluate, then do not worry so much about description. It may be helpful to underline or circle these terms as a reminder of where your focus should be.
- **Outline Your Answer First** Teachers are greatly influenced by the coherence and structure of your answer. To list facts in random order makes it seem as if you do not have a clear grasp of the material. Try to organize your answer prior to responding, including a strong topic sentence and 3-5 supporting details.
- **Take Time to Write an Introduction and Conclusion** A strong introduction and conclusion are essential parts of a good essay. They give your responses the structure of logical arguments.

True/False Tests

- Look for any word in the question that could make it false.
- Look out for extreme modifiers that tend to make a question false: all, none, never, only, etc.
- Identify qualifiers that tend to make questions true: usually, frequently, often, probably, etc

Multiple-Choice Tests

- Read each question with the intention of answering without looking at the possible answers. Decide in your mind what you think the answer is first.
- Underline key phrases in the question that may point to the correct answer.
- Always read all the choices before selecting.
- Use educated guessing: Eliminate two choices quickly and then decide between the remaining two.
- When in doubt, choose an answer in the middle range of the choices, rather than an extreme.

SUPPORTING ACADEMIC SUCCESS

Improving Academic Skills
Activity 29: Am I Prepped? Self-Evaluation

Appropriate For: GM, VM

Learning Objective:
The mentee will self-evaluate their test readiness.

Materials Needed:
Copies of "Am I Prepped? Self-Evaluation" worksheet, pen/pencil.

Instructions:
Ask your mentee to complete the evaluation below by putting a mark by each question that is true for them. Your mentee should be answering "yes" to all of these questions. Discuss any "no" responses and make a plan for incorporating this habit into practice or for their next assessment.

Am I Prepped? Self-Evaluation	
When preparing for a test, do you: • Concentrate on what you do not know? • Ask questions? • Ask your teacher for help, if necessary? • Create a study guide or flashcards?	• Get a good night's sleep before the test? • Make sure you know what will be covered? • Anticipate the questions your teacher is likely to ask? • Review any material from class or previous quizzes?
When taking a test, do you:	
• Read and understand the test directions? • Look over the entire test first? • Make sure you know how much time you are allotted? • Know how much each question counts for? • Notice key words in the directions or in specific questions? • Do the easiest questions first and return to the unanswered ones?	• Proofread your essay and/or short answers? • Watch out for careless mistakes? • Check that bubbles are filled in correctly when using a bubble sheet? • Write down important formulas, facts, or key words in the margin first so you will not forget them? • Pace yourself? • Read the whole question and all possible answers before selecting a response?
After taking a test, do you:	
Look for any grading mistakes? Look over the test and make sure that you understand your mistakes? Look up missed questions or ask a friend or the teacher for correct answers? Take notes when the teacher reviews the test in class? Save the test as study materials for future cumulative tests?	

Action Plan:

_____

_____

_____

_____

_____

_____

_____

_____

SUPPORTING ACADEMIC SUCCESS

Improving Academic Skills
Activity 30: Preparing for Standardized Tests

Appropriate For: GM, VM

Learning Objective:
The mentee will gain an understanding of effective preparation for all standardized tests.

Materials Needed:
Copies of "Standardized Test Prep Tips for Students" information sheet.

Instructions:
Share the tips below with your mentee as they begin to prepare a standardized test. Identify which tips they may already be using and which they could add to their repertoire. These tips may be particularly useful in helping students with testing anxiety feel more prepared. Helping your mentee prepare for their standardized tests can result in increased confidence, reduced anxiety, and better overall testing performance. If possible, provide them with a "Test Day Toolkit" to take in with them. The toolkit could include items such as pencils, erasers, a bottle of water, a pack of tissues, mints, and/or a "Good Luck" note.

Standardized Test Prep Tips for Students

Preparation Before the Test:

- Familiarize yourself with the content of the specific test.
- Refresh your knowledge and skills in the content areas.
- Take any and all practice tests that are available. There may be versions online in addition to the official practice tests put out by the testing company.
- Visit the test site's website to utilize the resources that may be available to you.
- Take advantage of any study groups that may be available at your school or in your community.
- Talk to friends or classmates who may have taken the test before to gain any helpful insights they may have.
- Know the different strategies for the specific tests; for example, knowing when it is best to give an educated guess or omit a question. (See Activities 23 & 24 in this toolkit for specific test-type tips.)
- If you have testing anxiety, make a game plan for what you will do if you start to feel nervous mid-test – for example, take ten deep breaths or close your eyes for a one-minute break.
- Get a good night's sleep the night before the test.

The Day of the Test:

- Eat a nutritious meal the night before and a healthy, low-sugar breakfast with protein, carbohydrates, and fruit the morning of – to jump-start your brain, keep yourself focused, and maintain energy.
- Take two sharpened #2 pencils and (if allowed) a calculator.

While Taking the Test:

- Read the test directions for each type of question at least twice before answering.
- Notice and underline key words in the directions.
- Make sure you know how much time is given per section.
- Pace yourself – do the easier questions first and return to the unanswered ones.
- Check your answer sheet regularly to make sure you are in the right place and that you have bubbled your answers correctly.

SUPPORTING ACADEMIC SUCCESS

Improving Academic Skills
Activity 31: Standardized Tests 101

Appropriate For: GM, VM

Learning Objective:
The mentee will gain an understanding of standardized tests and their registration procedures.

Materials needed:
Copies of "Standardized Tests 101," Internet access.

Instructions:
Standardized tests are used by colleges and universities to determine college admissions. Using the table below, work to familiarize your mentee with the different tests, including the preliminary tests that are available. Use the information to help them decide which test(s) make the most sense to register for. If your mentee already has ideas about which colleges and universities they would like to apply to, work together to check the school's website to see which test is required for admission. Also, be sure to remind your mentee to pay attention to registration requirements and dates.

Standardized Tests 101			
Test	**About the Test**	**Subject Matter**	**More Information**
PSAT/ NMSQT	• Provides feedback on a student's individual strengths and weaknesses in the different subject areas necessary for college and beyond. • Serves as a great indicator of what to expect on the SAT. • Is a requirement to be considered for the National Merit Scholarship, the National Hispanic Scholarship, and the National Negro Achievement Scholarship.	The test has three sections: Reading Test, Writing & Language Test, and Math Test. Many questions focus on important, widely used words and phrases. You'll be asked to interpret and use evidence. The math skills that matter most on the PSAT are problem solving, data analysis, and linear and complex equations.	Registration can only be done at your local high school. THERE IS NO ONLINE REGISTRATION OPTION AVAILABLE. To learn more about the test, including upcoming test dates, visit: https://collegereadiness.collegeboard.org/psat-nmsqt-psat-10 Fee waivers are available for 11th graders taking the PSAT/NMSQT, but there is no waiver available for PSAT 10 or PSAT 8/9.
SAT	• Helps to compare a student's academic knowledge with other students throughout the country. • Allows college admissions judges to evaluate your readiness for college. • There is no penalty for guessing on the new SAT. The test focuses on college- and career-ready knowledge and skills.	This is a 3-hour test made up of these sections: Evidence-Based Reading and Writing (100 minutes) Includes Reading Test and Writing and Language Test Math (80 minutes) Essay (Optional, 50 minutes)	For more on the SAT including registration, visit: https://collegereadiness.collegeboard.org/sat. Students may qualify for a fee waiver. Students who use a waiver for the SAT automatically receive four college application waivers.

Standardized Tests 101			
Test	**About the Test**	**Subject Matter**	**More Information**
Work Keys	• Demonstrates student readiness for various careers • The score and credential are recognized nationally by many major employers	The test measures three major areas and issues a nationally recognized career readiness certificate. • Applied Mathematics • Locating Information • Reading for Information • Students can also take additional sections that measure applied technology, business writing, listening for understanding, and workplace observation	WorkKeys is administered at assessment centers nationwide. To find a testing center, visit: http://www.act.org/content/act/en/products-and-services/workkeys-for-educators/shared/test-site-locator-form.html To learn more about WorkKeys, visit: http://www.act.org/content/act/en/products-and-services/workkeys-for-educators/assessments.html

Standardized Tests 101			
Test	**About the Test**	**Subject Matter**	**More Information**

ACT	• Helps to compare a student's academic knowledge with other students throughout the country
	
	• Allows college admissions judges to evaluate readiness for college
		This test is made up of the following sections:
		
		• English:
		
		  45 minutes, 75 questions
		
		  -Measures standard written English and rhetorical skills.
		
		• Mathematics:
		
		  60 minutes, 60 questions
		
		  -Measures mathematical skills typically acquired by the end of the 11th grade.
		
		• Reading:
		
		  35 minutes, 40 questions
		
		  -Measures reading comprehension
		
		• Science:
		
		  30 minutes, 40 questions
		
		  -Measures interpretation, analysis, evaluation, reasoning, and problem-solving skills.
		
		• Optional Writing Test: One prompt, 30 minutes
		
		  -Measures writing skills emphasized in high school English classes and in entry-level college composition courses.
			Registration for the ACT can be done via the internet or by mail. Students may qualify for a fee waiver, which has to be mailed in with the paper form of the ACT registration.
			
			To register by mail, students need to get the Student Registration Form from their school's guidance office. To register online, visit: www.act.org.

SECTION (4) COLLEGE READINESS

ACTIVITIES 32-39

Your mentee should begin to plan for college in as early in their high school career as possible. Your goal as a mentor is to get your mentee excited about the opportunity a post-secondary education will provide and assist with monitoring their progress toward college enrollment. The activities in this section are designed to help your mentee become familiar with and begin to prepare for the college transition process.

Preparing for College, Activities 32-37

This set of activities focuses on the college transition process, from becoming familiar with college terminology, to admissions procedures, to understanding the importance of a post-secondary education. These activities will be valuable to your mentee as they begin to compare and contrast college data when selecting which post-secondary institutions to apply to.

Financial Aid 101, Activities 38-39

Understanding the different forms of funding for college can be daunting. These activities provide information and resources that will inform your mentee about obtaining the various types of financial aid available.

Resource List:

The following websites may help you continue to explore college readiness with your mentee:

- **http://knowhow2go.acenet.edu/** – Offers numerous resources for college-bound high school students, including the 4 Steps to College and success stories of students who have achieved their post-secondary goals.
- **www.studentaid.ed.gov/sa/fafsa/estimate** – Allows younger students to use the FAFSA4Caster calculator to estimate what financial aid they are eligible for, based on current family income.
- **www.studentaid.ed.gov/sa/fafsa** – The primary source for FAFSA preparation and filing.
- **www.fastweb.com** – Allows students to perform free scholarship searches.

COLLEGE READINESS

Preparing for College
Activity 32: Why College?
Appropriate For: GM, VM

Learning Objective:
The mentee will gain an understanding of the importance of a post-secondary education.

Materials Needed:
Copy of "Why College?" worksheet, Internet access.

Instructions:
Ask your mentee to complete the statement below. Then review the benefits of attaining a post-secondary education with them via the "Why College?" information sheet. Does any of the information presented surprise them?

I think a post-secondary education is important/not important because...

Why College?

Money Talks

College graduates earn more than those who do not attain a post-secondary education. Every level of education attained beyond high school increases your income potential. According to the Bureau of Labor Statistics, the average annual earnings based on education levels are as follows:[1]

High School Dropout	$27,040
High School Diploma	$37,024
Some College, No Diploma	$40,248
Associate's Degree	$43,472
Bachelor's Degree	$60,996
Master's Degree	$72,852

This information can be viewed in graph form at **https://www.bls.gov/careeroutlook/2018/data-on-display/education-pays.htm**.

Job Security

The more education you achieve, the more likely it is you will always be employed. The Bureau of Labor Statistics also reports that the higher degree level attained, the lower the percentage of unemployment nationwide. For example, in 2018, the unemployment rate for individuals without a high school diploma was 6.5%, while the unemployment rate for individuals with a bachelor's degree was only 2.5%.

Impress the Boss

Continuing education after high school is much more important now than it was for previous generations. Today, most good jobs require more than a high school diploma. Businesses want to hire people who know how to think and solve problems, as well as effectively communicate both orally and in writing.

New Experiences

Education beyond high school provides you with many benefits beyond achieving your career goals, including meeting new people, taking part in different opportunities to explore your interests, and experiencing academic success.

---

1   Elka Torpey, "Measuring the value of education," Career Outlook, U.S. Bureau of Labor Statistics, April 2018.

COLLEGE READINESS

Preparing for College
Activity 33: Know Your Degrees

Appropriate For: GM, VM

Learning Objective:
The mentee will understand the value and meaning of the various post-secondary degrees.

Materials Needed:
Copy of "Know Your Degrees" information sheet, Internet access.

Instructions:
It is important for your mentee to understand the value and meaning of various post-secondary academic degrees. The specific degree awarded may depend on the school and the area of study. Review the information below to familiarize your mentee with this information. It may be helpful to share your own degree path and why you chose it. Ensure your mentee understands that the degrees listed below may not be offered at every college or university. Therefore, it is important to make sure that the degree(s) they are interested in align to the post-secondary institutions they are considering.

After reviewing this information, go to one of the following websites to check which degree is required for the career paths your mentee is considering:

- https://bigfuture.collegeboard.org/explore-careers/careers/matching-careers-to-degrees
- https://www.myplan.com/careers/database.html
- https://mycollegenavigationhub.com/career_degree/

Know Your Degrees

Doctoral Degree – the highest college degree awarded. It takes approximately five years to achieve and requires completing a course of study, original research, and a written, publishable thesis.

Master's Degree – awarded for successfully completing a graduate curriculum at a four-year college or university. Admission normally requires holding a bachelor's degree, although relevant work experience may be considered.

Bachelor's Degree – awarded for successfully completing an undergraduate curriculum at a four-year college or university. Course requirements and number of college credit hours will vary by program and institution, so it is important to review the requirements for programs you are particularly interested in. Degrees include:

- Bachelor of Arts (BA)
- Bachelor of Applied Science (BAS)
- Bachelor of Fine Arts (BFA)
- Bachelor of Science (BS)

Associate's Degree – awarded for successfully completing a course of study at a two-year college. It is designed to prepare students for progress toward a bachelor's degree or entry into the workforce. Degrees include:

- Associate in Arts (AA)
- Associate in Science (AS)
- Associate in Applied Science (AAS)

Certificate Programs – not considered college-level degree programs. Certificate programs prepare students for a position in a specific employment area and usually take one year or less to complete. Degrees include:

- Career and Technical Certificate (CTC)
- College Credit Certificate (CCC)

COLLEGE READINESS

Preparing for College
Activity 34: Ask the Admissions Counselor

Learning Objective:
The mentee will become familiar with the questions to ask an admissions counselor in order to make informed decisions in their college selection process.

Materials Needed:
Copies of "Ask the Admissions Counselor" worksheet, pen/pencil.

Instructions:
Admissions counselors have answers to the many questions a student may have about college. Review the questions listed on the "Ask the Admissions Counselor" information sheet. Then, use a mentoring session to practice having your mentee call the admissions office at the institution of their choice and get answers for their questions. It may be helpful to set up a phone appointment prior to the session to ensure a counselor is available.

Ask the Admissions Counselor	
Ask:	**Answer Provided:**
How big is the school?	
Are there any special requirements and deadlines for admission?	
What tests and what minimum scores does the school require?	
Is there an admission interview?	
How should I prepare for the interview?	
How much does it cost to attend school for one year, including tuition, room and board, and books?	
What types of financial assistance can I expect?	
How selective is the school?	
Where can I find information on the types of scholarships available?	
What is the ratio of faculty to students in most classes?	
What is the ratio of men to women?	
What are the most popular majors/ degree programs?	
Does the school have any areas of academic specialization?	
Are most students entering directly from high school or junior college, or returning to complete their education?	
What resources are available to students?	
What type of advisement or counseling do students receive?	
What extracurricular activities are available?	

COLLEGE READINESS

Preparing for College
Activity 35: College Application 101

Appropriate For: VM, GM

Learning Objective:
The mentee will gain an understanding of the basic information required to complete a college application.

Materials Needed:
Copy of "College Application 101" information sheet, Internet access.

Instructions:

Applying to college can be an overwhelming process for students. Below is a list of the sections generally included in a college application. Review this information with your mentee to help ease their concerns about the application process. If your mentee is a first-generation applicant, it may be useful to share this information with their parents as well. Once you have reviewed the information, help your mentee to research specific application requirements at the schools they are most interested in applying to.

College Application 101

How to Apply:

Students can apply to most college and universities in writing or online. Application information can be found on the school's website. Go to **https://searchenginesmarketer.com/company/resources/university-college-list/** for a database that lists most colleges and universities in the United States by state.

More and more schools are now accepting the Common Application, which allows students to complete one application and send it to multiple institutions. For a list of the schools that take the Common Application, go to **https://www.commonapp.org/explore-colleges**.

Application Forms:

Most schools have a specific application form they will ask you to fill out. This form will ask for basic information about you, such as contact information and information on your parents or guardian, as well as information that describes you as a student, such as schools attended and extracurricular activities participated in.

Fee:

The average college application fee is approximately $50-100. This fee is usually non-refundable, even if you are not accepted. Many colleges offer fee waivers for applicants who demonstrate financial need. If you need a fee waiver, see your school guidance counselor. If you received a fee waiver for either the SAT or ACT, you will probably be eligible for waivers from many schools.

High School Transcript:

Your high school transcript lists the classes you have taken and the grades you received. If your school uses class ranking, this information may be included as well. Most colleges require an official copy of the transcript, which means photo copies are not accepted and that your school will need to either send the transcript to the college directly OR will give you a copy in a sealed envelope that you can send yourself. Thus, you will need to speak directly with your school's guidance office to let them know which schools you need your transcripts sent to.

Admission Test Scores:

Many colleges require you to submit SAT or ACT test scores because they are a standard way of measuring a student's ability to do college work. When you complete your applications for the SAT and/or ACT, you can select the institutions to where you would like your results sent. You can also order copies of your score report sent after the fact at the test websites.

Letters of Recommendation:

Some colleges and universities ask you to submit one or more letters of recommendation from a teacher, counselor, coach, or other adult who knows you well. When asking someone to write such a letter, choose someone who can speak directly to your strengths as a student and as an individual. Be sure to ask the recommender well before the college's application deadline so they have time to draft a quality response. If needed, the website **https://eforms.com/recommendation-letter/ college**/ provides a free template as well as sample recommendations.

Personal Essay:

Many colleges also require students to submit written responses to one or more personal essay questions. The purpose of this section is to learn more about you as an individual, as well as assess your writing and communication skills. Some schools assign a topic, while others will give several choices for you to choose from. The length can vary as well, although most schools ask for 300-500 words. As with letters of recommendation, it is important not to wait until the last minute to draft your essay, as you will want at least one trusted adult to read your response and provide feedback.

COLLEGE READINESS

Preparing for College
Activity 36: College Application Dos and Don'ts

Appropriate For: GM

Learning Objective:
The mentee will gain a stronger understanding of the college application process.

Materials Needed:
Copies of "College Applications Dos and Don'ts" worksheet, blank college applications, pencils.

Instructions:
Review the "College Application Dos and Don'ts" with your mentee. Then work with your mentee to practice completing a blank paper application. You may also want to check if the schools your mentee is interested in take the Common Application, which allows students to apply to multiple schools with one application. For more on the Common Application, go to:

https://www.commonapp.org/.

For additional tips and resources, visit:

- http://www.educationplanner.org/students/preparing-for-school/apply/ten-tips.shtml
- https://bigfuture.collegeboard.org/get-in/applying-101/tips-for-preparing-your-college-application
- https://www.saraharberson.com/blog/ten-tips-on-filling-out-college-applications

College Application Dos and Don'ts

Do....

- Read all directions carefully.
- Apply online, if possible, so you are less likely to make careless errors.
- Have someone read and proofread all parts of your application to avoid typos.
- Use your essay as a chance to show admission officers your unique interests and qualities beyond academic skills.
- Include anything that makes you stand out from the crowd, such as honors, awards, or special talents.
- Review your high school transcript before you send it to colleges, making sure that it accurately reflects your courses, activities, awards, and grades.
- Find out if the college accepts special materials, such as a sample of your artwork.
- Make copies of everything you send.
- Submit application and supporting documents prior to due date/deadline.
- Keep track of when and where you send material (i.e., transcripts, application, essay)
- Call colleges to see if your application is complete and that they have received all of your documents.

Don't....

- Procrastinate.
- Lie or exaggerate with any information you provide.
- Leave out important details. For example, if you play in the school band, include what instrument you play.
- Submit a sloppy application.
- Borrow ideas for your essays, whether from a friend or a website.
- Go over the college's length limit for an essay. Admissions officers have limited time and many essays to review.
- Forget to follow-up once your application is sent. Write "thank you" letters to counselors, teachers, friends, or family who provided you with letters of recommendation.

COLLEGE READINESS

Preparing for College
Activity 37: Comparing Colleges

Appropriate For: VM, GM

Learning Objectives:
The mentee will compare and contrast college data to make an informed decision when selecting colleges to apply to.

Materials Needed:
Copies of "Comparing Colleges" worksheet, Internet access, pen/pencil.

Instructions:
Ask your mentee to identify their top three college choices, ranked in order of preference. Together, use the schools' websites or a college comparison website such as **https://bigfuture.college-board.org/compare-colleges** to complete the chart below. It may be useful to compare different types of schools (technical vs. 4-year, public vs private, etc.).

After you've compared schools, have your mentee re-rank them. Did the order of preference change? If so, what information was the deciding factor(s)? Were any schools eliminated based on the data collected? Use this information to start a list of other schools that also meet your mentee's most important criterion.

Comparing Colleges

	Choice #1 college name	Choice #2 college name	Choice #3 college name
Type (State College, 4-year University, Technical)			
Size Enrollment (# of students attending) • Size of Campus			
Environment • Urban, Rural, or Suburban • Co-ed or Single-Sex • Religious Affiliation			
Admission Requirements • Deadline • Tests Required • Average Test Scores • Average GPA • Average Rank of Student • Special Requirements			
Academics • Majors Offered • Special Requirements • Accreditation • Student-Faculty Ratio • Typical Class Size			
Expenses • Tuition • Room and Board • Estimated Total Budget • Application Fee			
Financial Aid • Deadline • Required Forms • % Receiving Aid • Scholarships			
Housing • Type of Housing Available • Most Students on Campus or Commuter • Meal Plan			
Facilities • Dormitories • Student Union • Religious • Parking			
Activities • Clubs • Greek Life • Other			
Other			

COLLEGE READINESS

Financial Aid 101
Activity 38: The Costs of College

Appropriate For: VM, GM

Learning Objective:
The mentee will become familiar with the costs of going to college.

Materials Needed:
Copies of "The Costs of College" budgeting worksheet, Internet access, pen/pencil.

Instructions:
With your mentee, visit the website for the college(s) they are most interested in and research the cost of attending. Help them complete the Cost of College budget form, using the data collected. This session may also be a good time to start discussing the importance of financial aid, including obtaining as many scholarships and grants as possible.

The Costs of College Budgeting Worksheet

COST (Per Semester)	School #1:	School #2:	School #3
Tuition			
Dorm or Rent			
Utilities			
Phone			
Internet			
Meal Plan or Groceries			
Books			
Fees (parking fees, lab fees, etc.)			
Computer Supplies			
Transportation (bus pass, gas, etc.)			
Insurance (car, health)			
Medical Expenses			
Other			
Total Cost of One Semester:			

COLLEGE READINESS

Financial Aid 101
Activity 39: Financial Aid Basics

Appropriate For: VM, GM

Learning Objective:
The mentee will gain a basic understanding of the different forms of funding for college.

Materials Needed:
Copies of "Financial Aid Basics" information sheet, Internet access, pen/pencil.

Instructions:
Research has shown that lack of funding is the top barrier many students face to enrolling in and/or completing their post-secondary education. Review the information on funding for college with your mentee to ensure they understand the basics. If your mentee is a first-generation college enrollee, it may be helpful to share this information with their parents as well. After you've reviewed the information, spend some time exploring the websites listed to see what financial aid opportunities might be available to your mentee.

Financial Aid Basics

Grants – A grant is money awarded to a student that does not have to repaid. It is usually based on financial need.

Scholarships – Scholarship money can be awarded because of academic achievement, outstanding talent or skill, and/or financial need. This money does not have to be repaid.

Loans – Loan monies are awarded to students on the condition that they are repaid within a specific amount of time.

Local Awards – High schools, churches, local businesses, and civic groups often sponsor financial aid programs that target talented students with demonstrated financial need from schools in their areas. Ask your guidance counselor about any local scholarship opportunities.

FAFSA – Stands for **F**ree **A**pplication for **F**ederal **S**tudent **A**id. The FAFSA form is the application students fill out to access federal and state money for college. The FAFSA can be completed on paper or online, and must be refiled every year a student is in college. It is always advised that students complete this form to be able to access all financial aid opportunities available to them. Furthermore, many schools (particularly public universities) require it.

College Work-Study – If you plan to work while in college, it is wise to explore work-study because any money earned will not count against you on your FAFSA application the following year.

Recommended Websites for Learning More About Financial Aid:

- **www.studentaid.ed.gov** – for information on all federal grant, scholarship, and loan programs
- **www.fafsa.ed.gov** – for more on the FAFSA and to complete the application online
- **http://knowhow2go.acenet.edu/middle-and-high-school-students/costs-and-financial-aid. html** – for more tips on affording college

SECTION 5 CAREER READINESS

Career Readiness
Activities 40-47

Discussing careers can be a very rewarding experience for you and your mentee. Using the career exploration tools in this section can be a great way for mentors to get their mentees motivated and excited about the future. Your goal as a mentor is to provide your mentee with practical information about working in the community. Remember, you are one of the "career experts" in your mentee's life – sharing your "real world" experiences will help prepare them for the world of work.

Entering the Work Force, Activities 40-41

These activities are designed to prepare your mentee to start reflecting on their readiness to enter the work force and choose a career path.

Career Exploration, Activities 42-47

These activities will assist mentees in gathering the information they need in order to make informed career path decisions. You can help guide your mentee in the right direction by ensuring they understand all the factors they should be take into consideration when making a career choice. You can also help your mentee build their own career skills and acquire valuable work experience as they prepare to enter the workforce.

Resource List:

The following websites may help you continue to explore careers with your mentee:

- **www.monster.com/career-advice** – Enables students to research careers. Also provides articles tailored specifically to students, such as finding summer-only positions.
- **www.linkedin.com/** – The world's most extensive career networking site.
- **www.careeronestop.org/toolkit** – Sponsored by the US Department of Labor, this site offers extensive career resources, including employment trends and projections, salary guides, and career exploration tests.
- **https://www.bls.gov/k12/students.htm** – The US Bureau of Labor Statistics' site for K-12 students. The site offers games and quizzes, in addition to informational articles sortable by grade level.

CAREER READINESS

Entering the Work Force
Activity 40: Am I Ready to Work?

Appropriate For: VM, GM

Learning Objective:
The mentee will self-assess their readiness for entering the work force.

Materials Needed:
Copies of "Am I Ready to Work?" self-assessment, pen/pencil.

Instructions:
Research has consistently shown that employers value executive functioning skills – that is, the skills that allow an individual to self-manage tasks, solve problems, and relate to others – more highly than specific content knowledge. Have your mentee complete the "Am I Ready to Work?" self-assessment. Discuss why each of the skills listed is important to the work setting. Then brainstorm an action plan for your mentee to improve upon one of the skills they find more challenging. Ask your mentee to complete the self-assessment below.

Am I Ready to Work?

On a scale of 1-5 (1= Never; 2 = Rarely; 3 = Sometimes; 4 = Usually; 5 = Always), how often do you:

Arrive on time to school/appointments?	
Ensure a neat appearance when leaving the house?	
Create and use a to-do list?	
Get along with others when working in a team?	
Proofread assignments before turning them in?	
Express concerns or frustrations in a calm manner?	
Listen to the concerns or frustrations of others in a calm manner?	
Remember to complete tasks assigned by my parents or teachers?	
Stay on-task when working alone on an assignment?	
Complete tasks even when tired or not feeling my best?	
Apply feedback given by my teachers, coaches, or parents?	
Make a plan for completing a project before starting?	
Stay focused in a long meeting or lecture?	
Accept changes to my schedule or plans in a calm manner?	
Respond to communications from others?	

CAREER READINESS

Entering the Work Force
Activity 41: My Career Priorities

Appropriate For: VM, GM

Learning Objective:
The mentee will explore their priorities and values when choosing a career pathway.

Materials Needed:
Copy of "My Career Priorities" worksheet, pen/pencil.

Instructions:
Ask your mentee to rank the items on the "My Career Priorities" sheet from 1 to 5, with 1 being the most important and 5 being the least important. Then discuss your mentee's answers with them. Ask them to elaborate on why they chose the rank they did for each item. Then talk about how different jobs may (or may not) align with their top priorities.

My Career Priorities

On a scale of 1-5 (1= Most Important; 2 = Very Important; 3 = Somewhat Important; 4 = Slightly Important; 5 = Not at All Important/Do Not Want), how would you rate the importance of each item on this list when choosing your ideal job? Mark your responses in the first column.

When you are done, review your responses. Did you assign any ranking more than 5 times? If so, re-do your rankings. This time, you can only give a particular ranking (1, 2, 3, 4, or 5) to five of the priorities listed. This will push you to very carefully consider what your highest (and lowest) priorities in a job really are!

PRIORITY	1st Ranking	2nd Ranking
High salary		
Good benefits (insurance, retirement, etc.)		
Ability to work from home		
Location convenient to your home		
Supervisor you enjoy working for		
Colleagues you enjoy working with		
Consistent 9-5 schedule		
A schedule that changes frequently		
Opportunities to travel		
Does not require travel		
Opportunity to learn/build new skills		
Opportunity to complete a degree		
A "fun" working environment		
A calm working environment		
A fast-paced working environment		
Opportunity for promotion/advancement		
A bigger corporation/organization with lots of employee opportunities		
A small-sized business/organization where you know and are comfortable with all of your colleagues		
Prestige/recognition in the community		

PRIORITY	1st Ranking	2nd Ranking
Job security		
Lots of opportunity for talking with customers or clients		
Requires very little interaction with customers or clients other than colleagues		
Work is mostly done in teams		
Work is mostly done solo		
Like/strongly believe in the company or organization's mission		

CAREER READINESS

Career Exploration
Activity 42: Gaining Work Experience

Appropriate For: VM, GM

Learning Objectives:
The mentee will learn about the different ways to gain work experience.

Materials Needed:
Copies of "Gaining Work Experience" information sheet, Internet access.

Instructions:
Gaining work experience can come in many different forms, from job shadowing to volunteering. Visit the websites provided below and review the information with your mentee. Which type of opportunity appeals to them most?

Gaining Work Experience

Gaining work experience early in your academic career can be a highly valuable investment in your future. Participation in volunteer projects, job shadowing, and/or a part-time job demonstrates a strong work ethic, a sense of community responsibility, and good character – to both college admissions committees and future employers. The information included below outlines the most common pathways for building your work experience while still in school.

JOB SHADOWING – www.jobshadow.com

Job shadowing includes spending time observing someone who is in a position you would like to learn more about. This site provides information on what job shadowing is, as well as contacts for those who are interested in participating in a job shadow program. Let your guidance counselor know that you are interested in job shadowing to find out more about opportunities your school or community may have.

PART-TIME JOB

Part-time jobs are convenient for students, giving them the opportunity to work a few hours after school, on the weekends, or during the summer and other school breaks. A part-time job should not interfere with your studies. Speak with your guidance counselor to find out more about part-time jobs that may be available to you. The following sites all have searchable databases that allow you to browse part-time jobs in your local area.

- www.monster.com
- www.indeed.com
- www.snagajob.com

VOLUNTEER PROJECTS – www.volunteermatch.org

Volunteer projects are a great way for you to build a strong record of achievement, community service, and leadership. Students who volunteer for a wide variety of community projects will be exposed to many different types of business and civic organizations. You will also meet community and business leaders who can assist you in your future career. This site is a resource to find more information about volunteer opportunities in your community.

You can get more information about opportunities for work experience from:

- Your school's guidance department
- Local Chamber of Commerce
- Civic and business organizations

CAREER READINESS

Career Exploration
Activity 43: Creating a Cover Letter

Appropriate For: VM, GM

Learning Objective:
The mentee will learn how to construct a cover letter.

Materials Needed:
Copies of "Creating a Cover Letter" information sheet, lined paper (or chart paper if in a group setting), pens or markers, Internet access.

Instructions:
Review the "Creating a Cover Letter" information sheet to help your mentee understand the purpose of a cover letter and how to construct one. Then, work with them to create their own cover letter on a separate piece of paper. In a group setting, this could be done collectively using chart paper.

You can view sample cover letters for students, as well as templates for constructing a cover letter, online at:

www.thebalancecareers.com/student-cover-letter-samples-2063664

www.resumegenius.com/cover-letter-examples/college-student-cover-letter-sample

Creating a Cover Letter

A cover letter expresses specifically how your skills and experiences will benefit the company or position to which you are applying. See below for a basic cover letter format.

Your Name: Include your full name and mailing address.

Date: Use today's date.

Address: Address your letter to a specific person at a specific company. If you are unaware of the person's name, be sure to state the name of the department.

Salutation: This letter should be written to whom you have addressed it. If you are unaware of the individual's name, an alternative could be "Hiring Committee" or "Human Resource Manager."

Body: This should include three paragraphs:

- **1ST** Should demonstrate how your experiences align with the position to which you are applying and establish a connection to the company's goals and objectives.
- **2ND** Should state your top skills and highlight the benefits you will bring to the company.
- **3RD** Should initiate action by explaining what you will do next (e.g., follow up) or prompt the employer to contact you to set up an interview. Close with a "Thank you."

Closure: "Sincerely" or "Respectfully" works well.

Signature: Allow space for your handwritten signature, and type in your full name below it.

CAREER READINESS

Career Exploration
Activity 44: A Winning Resume

Appropriate For: VM

Learning Objective:
The mentee will learn how to create an effective resume.

Materials Needed:
Copies of "A Winning Resume" information sheet, lined paper and pens, OR Internet access.

Instructions:
Constructing a solid resume is the first step to attaining a job. Review the "A Winning Resume" information sheet below with your mentee. On a separate piece of paper, help them draft their own resume, based on their experiences and previous jobs. This can also be done online, using a free resume builder such as **www.resumegenius.com** or **https://studentedge.org/jobs/resume-builder.**

You can view sample student resumes at:

https://www.thebalancecareers.com/student-resume-examples-and-templates-2063555

https://www.hloom.com/resumes/high-school-graduate-templates/

A Winning Resume

Let your resume represent the best YOU, highlighting your education, experiences, and unique qualities. Below is a basic resume format.

Your Contact Information: Include your full name, full address, telephone number, and email address. If you have a LinkedIn profile, include that as well.

Objective (optional): Link your skills and experience with those required by the company. Focus on the goals of the organization and how you address them.

Career Highlights/Qualifications (optional): List career-related achievements, skills, traits, and experience relevant to the position for which you are applying. It lets the prospective employer know how you are qualified for the job.

Experience: Include your work history (paid and volunteer). List the company's name; dates of employment, in order of most recent first; the positions you held; and a bulleted list of what you did for your employer/volunteer organization/community.

Education: List the school(s) you have attended; the dates of attendance, in order of most recent first; the degrees you attained; and any special awards and/or honors you earned. Note any honors-level or Advanced Placement coursework as well.

Skills and Personal Interests: List the skills related to the position/career field for which you are applying, i.e., computer or technical skills, athletic abilities, or other talents.

Honors/Awards: List any pertinent honors/awards you have received that show your qualification for the position.

Languages: List languages you speak, read, and/or write along with the level of proficiency.

CAREER READINESS

Career Exploration
Activity 45: Getting the Job

Appropriate For: VM

Learning Objective:
The mentee will gain an understanding of the job search and application process.

Materials Needed:
Copies of "Getting the Job" information sheet

Instructions:
Review the information in the "Getting the Job" information sheet to help your mentee understand the job search and application process. This is a great opportunity to share your own professional experiences with them, both successes and challenges.

Getting the Job

Step 1: Find a job that interests you

In today's world, jobs are listed in a variety of ways: Internet job sites, ads, on the web, classified posts, on school campus, and company websites. Start your search using one of these methods and keep a list of the positions that interest you. The following websites are databases that include part-time jobs for students, as well as full-time positions:

- www.monster.com
- www.indeed.com
- www.snagajob.com

Step 2: Inquire about the position

Once you have selected several positions that interest you, proceed by contacting the company/organization and inquiring about the position. Is the position still open? Is there an application to complete? To whom can you forward your resume and cover letter? Usually a simple email to the Human Resources department or contact will suffice.

Step 3: Provide the potential employer with your cover letter and resume

Refer to Activities 43 and 44 for cover letter and resume format.

Remember that your cover letter and resume are a reflection of who you are, so make sure they have been proofread and are free of errors. In today's world of social media, you will also want to ensure that any viewable pages or feeds are work-appropriate – potential employers have been known to check! Once your application is submitted, you should receive confirmation that it was received. If not, it is fine to take the initiative to call/email and politely inquire.

If granted an interview, see Activity 46 for Interviewing Tips!

CAREER READINESS

Career Exploration
Activity 46: Interviewing Tips 101

Appropriate For: VM, GM

Learning Objective:
The mentee will learn and practice tips for successfully navigating a job interview.

Materials Needed:
Copies of "Interviewing Tips 101" information sheet.

Instructions:
A successful job interview requires preparation, professionalism, and follow-up.

Review the tips below with your mentee to prepare them for a successful interview experience. You may wish to combine this activity with Activity 47 – "Mock Interview."

INTERVIEWING TIPS 101

Before Your Interview

- Research the company and become well informed on their mission, goals, and future plans.
- Prepare ahead by anticipating questions that may be asked of you.
- Prepare questions you want to ask during the interview. Make sure they aren't questions whose answers can be easily found on the company website.
- Make sure your clothes are business-like, clean, pressed, and conservative. Make sure your hair and nails are trimmed and clean.
- Bring a fresh copy of your resume and a notepad to take notes.

During Your Interview

- Be on time; better yet, arrive 10-15 minutes early.
- Extend your hand when you are being greeted and shake hands firmly. Treat everyone you encounter with respect.
- Make eye contact with your interviewer and smile when appropriate. Do not sit until you are invited to do so.
- Be positive and avoid any negative comments about past employers.
- If you have unanswered questions, wait and ask them when appropriate. This will show your interest and ability to think critically.
- Listen carefully. If you feel the question is unclear, ask politely for clarification. Pause before answering to consider all facts that may substantiate your response. Discuss only the facts needed to respond to the question.
- Focus and re-focus attention on your successes. Remember, the goal is not to have the right answers so much as it is to convince the interviewer that you are the right person.
- Be truthful, but try not to offer unsolicited information.
- Try not to open yourself to areas of questioning that could pose difficulties for you.

After Your Interview

- Send a brief "Thank You" email to the individual(s) who interviewed you. Summarize the points you made in your interview or add a brief but crucial point that you might have forgotten.
- Do NOT press the employer for a decision. If the employer said they would have a decision in a week, it is okay to call or email them in a week to thank them for the interview and reiterate your interest.
- If you receive word that another candidate was chosen, you may send a follow-up letter to the employer, thanking them for the opportunity to interview for the position. Let them know that, should another or similar position open in the future, you would be interested in interviewing again.

CAREER READINESS

Career Exploration
Activity 47: Mock Interview

Appropriate For: VM, GM

Learning Objective:
The mentee will become familiar with potential interview questions through a mock interview.

Materials Needed:
Paper, pen/pencil.

Instructions:
Preparing for an interview requires anticipating questions that may be asked by a potential employer. These questions may require your mentee to formulate well thought out responses. (This activity is great for preparing for college interviews as well!) Inform your mentee that there are no right or wrong answers, and that a prepared response may impress the potential employer. Help your mentee become comfortable with the interview process by drafting potential responses to some common interview questions, and then conducting a mock interview, where they have an opportunity to present the responses planned.

Questions to Consider:

- Tell me about yourself.
- What are your greatest strengths as an employee?
- What are your greatest challenges as an employee?
- Why do you think you are the best candidate for this position?
- Can you describe a challenge you have encountered and how you overcame it?
- What is something that you have accomplished that you are very proud of?
- Where do you see yourself in five years?
- How do you handle conflict?
- What motivates you to put forth the greatest effort?
- Have you ever had difficulty with a supervisor or teacher? If so, please explain the issue and how it was resolved.

Feel free to share your personal interviewing experiences with your mentee throughout this process!

SECTION (6) ROAD MAP TO COLLEGE

Activities 48-53

Planning for High School Graduation

The activities in this section are designed to help your mentee with their educational planning for each year of middle and high school. Planning tasks include identifying the right courses to take and preparing for standardized tests. Your goal as a mentor is to assist your mentee in tracking their progress toward high school graduation and their college and career goals.

ROAD MAP TO COLLEGE

Planning for High School Graduation
Activity 48: Checklist – Middle School

Learning Objective:
The mentee will follow the recommended suggestions for college-/career-bound freshmen.

Materials Needed:
Copy of "Checklist - Middle School" worksheet, pen/pencil.

Instructions:
Review the checklist with your middle school mentee. Keep a copy of this list in a safe place and allow them to check off each task as they complete it. Building a college-bound mindset will help your mentee on the road to college and future success even while still in middle school. Feel free to add any additional steps you find are helpful for your mentee along the way!

Checklist – Middle School

- Research high schools in your area and special programs they may offer.
- Take the most challenging math class you can handle.
- Get involved in school- or community-based extracurricular activities.
- Start reading magazine and newspaper articles on topics that interest you.
- Keep a journal to develop good writing skills.
- Ask your counselor about challenging and interesting courses you could take.
- Consider volunteering in your community.
- Talk to older siblings or other young people you know who are attending college about their experience, and any insight they wish they had known in middle school!

ROAD MAP TO COLLEGE

Planning for High School Graduation
Activity 49: Graduation Requirements

Learning Objective:

The mentee will create an outline of the courses they will need to complete to stay on track for high school graduation.

Materials Needed:

Copies of "Graduation Requirements" worksheet, pen/pencil, Internet access.

Instructions:

Students are required to complete a certain number of courses on their road to high school graduation. You can find this information at your state's Department of Education website. Go to this link for a list of each state's DOE web address: **https://www2.ed.gov/about/contacts/state/index.html**.

In order to ensure that your mentee is on track for graduation, assist them with outlining their course plan. Use the attached chart to note the number of credits your mentee needs to earn in each subject area, and courses they may wish to take each year to meet the requirement.

ROAD MAP TO HIGH SCHOOL GRADUATION

Subject Area	Required Credits	Freshman Course(s)	Sophomore Course(s)	Junior Course(s)	Senior Course(s)
English					
Mathematics					
History/ Social Studies					
Science					
Art					
Foreign Language					
Physical Education/ Health					
Electives					
Community Service Requirement					

Keep this list in a safe place and refer back to it annually. This will be a good way to ensure that you are on the right path toward graduating on time.

ROAD MAP TO COLLEGE

Planning for High School Graduation
Activity 50: Checklist – Freshman Year

Learning Objective:
The mentee will follow the recommended suggestions for college-/career-bound freshmen.

Materials Needed:
Copies of "Checklist – Freshman Year" worksheet, pen/pencil.

Instructions:
Review the checklist with your freshman mentee. Keep a copy of this list in a safe place and allow them to check off each task as they complete it.

Checklist – Freshman Year

- Create a GPA goal – check-in every semester or quarter to see if you are on-track.
- Choose a sport or club at school to join
- If required, start working on your community service hours.
- Create a high school resume and include your awards, achievements, paid and/or volunteer work, extracurricular activities, classes taken, fluent language(s), and technical skills.
- Explore career options.
- Start preparing for the PSAT.

ROAD MAP TO COLLEGE

Planning for High School Graduation
Activity 51: Checklist – Sophomore Year

Learning Objective:
The mentee will follow the recommended suggestions for college-/career-bound sophomores.

Materials Needed:
Copies of "Checklist – Sophomore Year" worksheet, pen/pencil.

Instructions:
Review the checklist regularly with your sophomore mentee.

Checklist – Sophomore Year

- Continue to set and monitor a GPA goal.
- Print out HS graduation requirements
- Begin thinking about an internship experience or career shadowing opportunity
- Take PSAT.
- Begin to research colleges, college fairs, and summer program offerings at colleges
- Use the FAFSA 4Caster to estimate the amount of need-based financial aid you'll be eligible for (https://fafsa.ed.gov/spa/fafsa4c/?locale=en_US#/landing).
- Narrow down top colleges and universities to coincide with your interested area of study.
- Research standardized tests and requirements of these top schools.
- Update HS resume w/awards, achievements, clubs. Continue participating in extracurricular activities and sports – seek out leadership roles.
- Participate in college tours when possible (some schools offer virtual tours on their websites!).

ROAD MAP TO COLLEGE

Planning for High School Graduation
Activity 52: Checklist – Junior Year

Learning Objective:
The mentee will follow the recommended suggestions for college-/career-bound juniors.

Materials Needed:
Copies of "Checklist – Junior Year" worksheet, pen/pencil.

Instructions:
Review the checklist regularly with your junior mentee.

Checklist – Junior Year

- Take as many AP and Dual Enrollment classes as you can comfortably take pertaining to a proposed major. Be sure to consult with a college advisor and high school counselor.
- Continue to set and monitor a GPA goal
- Sign up for SAT/ACT.
- Take a deeper dive into college/university list of requirements for application: i.e., ACT, SAT scores, essays, letters of reference.
- SAT/ACT; begin preparing for test.
- Research scholarships and grants you would qualify for.
- Update HS resume w/awards, achievements, work experience, and leadership roles. Continue participating in extracurricular activities and sports – seek out leadership roles.
- Continue to earn and record volunteer/community service hours.
- Participate in college tours, and research summer program offerings at colleges.
- Over the summer, start filling out college applications. If you qualified for a SAT/ACT fee waiver, you will receive application fee waivers as well.

ROAD MAP TO COLLEGE

Planning for High School Graduation
Activity 53: Checklist - Senior Year

Learning Objective:
The mentee will follow the recommended suggestions for college-/career-bound seniors.

Materials Needed:
Copies of "Checklist – Senior Year" worksheet, pen/pencil.

Instructions:
Review the checklist regularly with your senior mentee.

Checklist – Senior Year

- Take as many AP and Dual Enrollment classes as you can comfortably take pertaining to a proposed major. Be sure to consult with a college advisor and high school counselor.
- Continue to set and monitor a GPA goal.
- Retake the SAT/ACT if necessary.
- Update HS resume w/awards, achievements, work experience, and leadership roles
- Track application deadlines for the colleges you are interested in applying to. Make sure you are aware of each school's application process, including essay/biographical requirements, average GPA, exam requirements, recommendation requirements, etc. If you feel strongly about a school, consider applying for early admission.
- Arrange to have your SAT/ACT scores sent to every school you may want to attend. Your scores will be updated every time you retake an exam, and this will get you on their mailing list.
- Practice writing essays.
- Ask teachers, coaches, and other adults who know you well to write recommendation letters.
- Complete the FAFSA workshop.
- Complete applications for schools you are interested in. Don't forget to apply for a fee waiver if you qualify.

Introduction

Group mentoring is one method for providing mentors and mentees the experience and benefits of the traditional 1:1 mentoring model, using fewer resources. When implemented appropriately, the group mentoring model can empower students to become advocates for their own success by sharing information and offering advice, social support, coaching, and counseling. Other benefits of the group mentoring model include a reduced need for mentors (particularly useful for mentoring organizations that struggle to find qualified volunteers), richer mentoring session discussions (aided by more varied perspectives and insights), and peer-to-peer support the mentees can provide one another.

Benefits of the Group Mentoring Model
✓ Provides service to more mentees, using fewer resources
✓ Reduced need for volunteer mentors
✓ Richer mentor session discussions – more perspectives included
✓ Peer-to-peer support

Before implementing the Group Mentoring model, it is important to be aware of the associated challenges as well. For example, there may be students who cannot or should not be paired together due to personality conflicts. Mentees with quieter or more introverted personalities may be more successful sharing their insights one-on-one, rather than in a group. Group mentoring sessions can also be logistically challenging to plan, since a bigger location is needed and numerous schedules have to be considered. However, if these considerations can be successfully navigated, this model can be a highly effective means for mentoring organizations to achieve their goals.

Implementing the Group Mentoring Model

Take Stock in Children allows their network affiliates to utilize the group mentoring model and has carefully documented the process for successful implementation. The graphic below outlines this process for organizations interested in this practice, while Table 1 provides further detail on each step of the process.

Process for Implementing the Group Mentor Model

Table 1

Process Step	To Consider
Assess Readiness	Does your program have access to: • Groups of students that can be easily clustered for a common meeting time and location • Access to mentors experienced with managing groups of students (teachers and coaches make great group mentors!) • Program staff that can effectively group students based on individual characteristics • Space that can accommodate group meetings and coordinated scheduling efforts
Recruit and Train Mentors	Mentors Should: • Meet program qualifications for safety and security • Have experience working with groups of students • Examples include teachers, coaches, scout leaders, clergy members, and youth group leaders
Group Students for Maximum Effectiveness	When grouping students, program staff should consider: • Personality-type of mentor and mentees • Shared experiences and /or goals • Interest commonalities • Schedule/Location availability • It is also important to consider the size of each group. No more than 6 students per group is ideal.

Set Expectations and Conduct Sessions	Prior to beginning sessions, program staff should work with mentors to address the following: • Curriculum to use (Note: the exercises in the Mentor Toolkit coded as GM have been identified as easily adaptable for a group setting) • Schedule/Location (Should be easily accessible to all participants) • A process for adopting group norms and expectations (Should be developed in conjunction with mentees) • Roles and responsibilities • Any necessary program requirements related to safety and security
Monitor and Refine the Model as Needed	In early implementation of a new model, it is important for program staff to check in frequently with mentors and mentees to assess the following questions: • Is the group mentoring model working as planned? • Are there any group or individual challenges that need to be addressed? • Is the group model sufficient to meet mentee needs and address mentee goals, or are some 1:1 sessions required as well? • Do any changes need to be made to the schedule, location, or curriculum?

Group Mentoring Curriculum

As noted above, certain activities in the College and Career Readiness Mentor Toolkit have been designated as appropriate for and easily adaptable to a group setting. These activities can be identified by the code **GM**. However, mentors may wish to design additional sessions to supplement the activities provided here. This section provides guidance in how to plan a mentoring session. **Please note, mentors should always obtain approval from their affiliated organization before deviating from an approved curriculum.**

How to Design a Group Mentor Session

State the Objective → Investigate Activity Options → Plan Realistic Timing → Write Down a Plan

Design Steps

Planning a group mentoring session is very similar to designing a lesson plan that might be implemented in a classroom setting. Mentors should follow these steps when determining what to include in and how to approach a session. Mentors with previous educational experience may have lesson plan development techniques that work for them, but a good rule of thumb is to always produce a written plan as a guide.

1. **State the Objective**—Mentors should ask themselves what they want their students to learn or gain from the mentoring session.

2. **Investigate Activity Options**—The Internet is a vast resource full of free advice and ideas for conducting effective mentor sessions. Google searches on specific topics can also direct mentors to ideal activities that fit the stated objective.

3. **Plan Realistic Timing**—One of the most challenging aspects of planning a lesson or mentor session is making sure that the planned activities fit comfortably within the session's timeframe. When timing goes awry, it is usually because there was too much activity or content packed into a session. It's better to end early or plan for an intentional pause so that a topic can be continued next session rather than not getting to the core content of a lesson. This being said, there could be instances where an early part of a discussion leads to an incredibly rich and meaningful conversation that was not planned. In cases like this, mentors use their best judgment about how to revise their plan in response to student need.

4. **Write Down a Plan**—The following structure is suggested to help mentors organize and record their plan for a mentor session. It can be used to record the session objective, introduction, main activity, resources and materials, informal assessment, and closure.

Group Mentor Session Structure

Topic: This is the title of your session and should reflect the guiding principle and objective in an abbreviated way.

Objective: This critical piece of planning defines the session and sets the stage for success. No matter how fun or important a session activity is, without a clear objective, it misses the mark.

Resources/Materials: List all resources and materials needed for a successful session. Nothing is worse than having a well-planed session only to find that important materials are missing when the time comes to use them.

Introduction: Give mentees a '30,000 foot' view of the session – i.e. what they will be discussing and an overview of what is expected of them. This is also an opportunity to activate prior knowledge and find out what students already know about a topic.

Main Activity: This is the core of the mentor session, where you are directly coaching the mentees. Be sure that whatever activity is chosen reflects what the mentees already know and what you want to teach them.

Assessment: Every mentor session should include an informal or anecdotal assessment. This is a way for mentors to check student understanding and find out if additional support is needed.

Closure: Every session should have an opportunity to summarize or wrap up the discussion. Examples of this include asking mentees to: write a sentence about what they learned, briefly state what they liked/disliked about the session, or make suggestions for follow-up topics and activities.

Further Resources

For more on Group Mentoring, please go to the following resources:

- **www.takestockinchildren.org** – Go to the TSIC website to purchase a copy of the Group Mentoring implementation manual.
- **www.nationalmentoringresourcecenter.org** – Offers information as well as current research on the group mentoring model.
- **www.mentoring.org** – Also offers information on implementing the group mentoring model.

Introduction

Virtual mentoring is an alternative form of mentoring where participants primarily rely on electronic tools to communicate. Virtual mentoring is based on a mutually beneficial relationship between a mentor and a student, with the mentor providing the student with knowledge, advice, encouragement, and skill modeling. Some mentoring organizations may allow all sessions to be conducted virtually, while others (such as Take Stock in Children) use virtual mentoring as a supplement to the traditional, in-person model. Due to safety and security concerns, many programs require virtual mentoring sessions to use supervised video conferencing through platforms such as GoBoard.com. Mentors should always obtain approval from their associated organization before implementing a virtual mentoring model.

When implemented thoughtfully and appropriately, there are multiple benefits to utilizing the virtual mentoring model. First and foremost, this model removes potential barriers to regular contact between mentors and mentees. Using virtual mentoring, mentor-mentee sessions can occur consistently throughout the year, even when geographical, time, or financial constraints hinder in-person meetings. Virtual mentoring has a very low barrier to entry, requiring only Internet access (and access to a virtual platform if designated by the mentoring organization). Virtual mentoring also provides opportunity for a more diverse body of mentors, since scheduling and geographic concerns are minimized. As a result, organizations may be able to greatly increase their rate of mentor-mentee pairings by allowing the virtual mentoring model.

Benefits to the Virtual Mentoring Model

✓ Removal of Barriers to Regular Contact

✓ Opportunity for More Diverse Mentors

✓ Increased Mentor Match Rate

When considering whether to implement the virtual mentoring model, it is important to consider the challenges as well. The biggest concern for mentoring organizations using virtual mentoring is ensuring the safety and security of both mentors and mentees. The Internet is vast, and regulation of mentor-mentee contact can be more difficult.

To ensure that online communication between mentors and students is appropriate, programs should consider taking extra steps to ensure that safety. For example, Take Stock in Children requires all virtual mentoring sessions to take place at a TSIC-sanctioned location, with supervision from a

TSIC staff member (or other designated person). Additionally, all TSIC virtual mentoring sessions must be recorded and stored using the GoBoard virtual platform.

Given the nature of security requirements, the increased need for technical literacy is another potential challenge of this model. While most virtual platforms are fairly user-friendly, mentors and mentees must both have basic computer skills, as well as consistent access to an internet-enabled computer.

Finally, organizations considering virtual mentoring should be aware of and plan to address the potential for miscommunication between mentors and mentees. While online communication is efficient, it can also invite misunderstanding. When virtually mentoring, it is especially important for mentors and mentees to be considerate and thoughtful about communication as the person they are communicating with is not physically in the room. It may require some targeted effort to overcome the digital divide. Communication can also be negatively impacted by technical issues, such as limited sound quality, broadband issues causing downtime, and connectivity issues.

Implementing the Virtual Mentoring Model

Take Stock in Children allows their network affiliates to utilize the virtual mentoring model and has carefully documented the process for successful implementation. The graphic below outlines this process for organizations interested in this practice, while Table 1 provides further detail on each step of the process.

Process for Implementing the Virtual Mentor Model

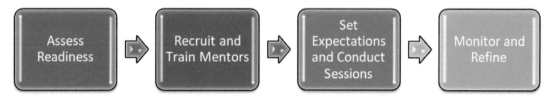

Table 1

Process Step	To Consider
Assess Readiness	Does your program have access to: • Mentors/mentees with the technical knowledge to take part in virtual mentoring • Access to internet-enabled computers with microphones and headphones • Access to virtual platform software such as GoBoard (highly recommended) • Program or designated staff available to supervise virtual sessions and assist with technical difficulties (highly recommended) • The capacity to monitor and/or record virtual mentoring sessions (necessary for safety purposes)
Recruit and Train Mentors	Mentors should: • Meet program qualifications for safety and security • Possess basic computer skills and have an active interest in virtual mentoring • Be willing and able to follow all program safety requirements, such as only communicating with students at approved times and locations through approved means
Set Expectations and Conduct Sessions	Prior to beginning sessions, program staff should work with mentors to address the following: • Curriculum to use (Note: the exercises in the Mentor Toolkit coded as **VM** have been identified as easily adaptable for a virtual setting) • Schedule/Location (Needs to work with the mentor and mentee's schedule and allow for designated staff to supervise) • Access to all necessary equipment and software for both mentor and mentee • A process for introducing and enforcing all related safety measures (such as use of a virtual platform and only communicating via sanctioned means)

Monitor and Refine the Model as Needed	In early implementation of a new model, it is important for program staff to check in frequently with mentors and mentees to assess the following questions: • Is the virtual mentoring model working as planned? • Are there any challenges that need to be addressed? • Is the virtual model sufficient to meet mentee needs and address mentee goals, or are some in-person sessions required as well? • Do any changes need to be made to the schedule, location, or curriculum?

Virtual Mentoring Curriculum

As noted above, certain activities in the College and Career Readiness Mentor Toolkit have been designated as appropriate for and easily adaptable to a virtual setting. These activities can be identified by the code **VM**. However, mentors may wish to design additional sessions to supplement the activities provided here. This section provides guidance in how to plan a mentoring session. **Please note, mentors should always obtain approval from their affiliated organization before deviating from an approved curriculum.**

How to Design a Virtual Mentoring Session

State the Objective > Investigate Activity Options > Plan Realistic Timing > Write Down a Plan

Design Steps

Planning a virtual mentoring session is very similar to designing a lesson plan that might be implemented in a classroom setting. Mentors should follow these steps when determining what to include in and how to approach a session. Mentors with previous educational experience may have lesson plan development techniques that work for them, but a good rule of thumb is to always produce a written plan as a guide.

1. **State the Objective**—Mentors should ask themselves what they want their students to learn or gain from the mentoring session.

2. **Investigate Activity Options**—The Internet is a vast resource full of free advice and ideas for conducting effective mentor sessions. Additionally, Google searches on specific topics can also direct mentors to ideal activities that fit the desired objective.

3. **Plan Realistic Timing**—One of the most challenging aspects of planning a mentor session is making sure that the planned activities fit comfortably within the session's timeframe. When timing goes awry, it is usually because there was too much activity or content packed into a session. It's better to end early or plan for an intentional pause so that a topic can be continued next session rather than not getting to the core content of a lesson. This being said, there could be instances where an early part of a discussion leads to an incredibly rich and meaningful conversation that was not planned. In cases like this, mentors use their best judgment about how to revise their plan in response to student need.

4. **Write Down a Plan**—The following structure is suggested to help mentors organize and record their plan for a mentor session. It can be used to record the session objective, introduction, main activity, resources and materials, informal assessment, and closure.

Virtual Mentor Session Structure

Topic: This is the title of your session and should reflect the guiding principle and objective in an abbreviated way.

Objective: This critical piece of planning defines the session and sets the stage for success. No matter how fun or important a session activity is, without a clear objective, it misses the mark.

Resources/Materials: List all resources and materials needed for a successful session. Nothing is worse than having a well-planed session only to find that important materials are missing when the time comes to use them. Remember to make sure the materials you plan to use are compatible with the online platform you are using.

Introduction: Give mentees a "30,000-foot" view of the session – i.e., what they will be discussing and an overview of what is expected of them. This is also an opportunity to activate prior knowledge and find out what students already know about a topic.

Main Activity: This is the core of the mentor session, where you are directly coaching the mentees. Be sure that whatever activity is chosen reflects what the mentees already know and what you want to teach them.

Assessment: Every mentor session should include an informal or anecdotal assessment. This is a way for mentors to check student understanding and find out if additional support is needed.

Closure: Every session should have an opportunity to summarize or wrap up the discussion. Examples of this include asking mentees to: write a sentence about what they learned, briefly state what they liked/disliked about the session, or make suggestions for follow-up topics and activities.

Further Resources

For more on Virtual Mentoring, please go to the following resources:

- **www.takestockinchildren.org** – Go to the TSIC website to purchase a copy of the Virtual Mentoring implementation manual.
- **https://artofmentoring.net/virtual-mentoring/** – Offers insight into implementing a virtual mentoring model.